7 STEPS TO YOUR
RADICAL
AWAKENING

Find the Calm in the Storm of Overwhelm

RAMANA

Book illustrations: by Cheryl Bennett and Katie van Munster

Cover design: inspired by Lulu Love Rose, and executed by Ella Stok- Iachetti

Photo credit: Hubble Telescope, Cat-eye nebula

About the Cover: *When we look out from the cave of the heart, we see the vision of our True Self is as an infinite universe.*

For permission requests, write to the publisher, addressed "Attention: Permissions Coordinator," at the address below.

Radical Awakening Seminars

61 Grand Ave, Rochester, NY 14609

or email ramana@radicalawakening.org

www.radicalawakening.org

Link to Audio Files that Take You Through
The *Radical Awakening* Process

http://tinyurl.com/jjwtqew

IMPORTANT: refer to *How to Use this Book*,
which follows the *Introduction*, for detailed
instructions about downloading files.

Notes on the 2nd Edition:

What started out to be a revision, in the end, turned out to be a major rewrite of most of the book. The 2nd Edition of this book not only includes many new chapters, but the 7 Steps to Radical Awakening scripts has been reworded, and all of the recordings have been re-done. Please enjoy the fruits of a year and a half I spent in this revision!

Live life as if everything is aligned in your favor.

– Rumi

This book is dedicated to my mother, Grace,
whose strength, thoughtfulness and generosity of heart
were an inspiration to every life she touched.

December 1925 – December 2017

The holy mountain Arunachala, India

Sri Ramana Maharshi

December 1879 – April 1950

H. W. L. Poonja (Papaji)

October 1910 - September 1997

Author's Preface

As early as I can remember, I felt in my heart that there was more to life than what the world was presenting me. I had an inner knowing that there was a presence, an inner universe, that transcended my unsatisfying life. There were no words to explain it and no one I could talk to about it so I embarked on a journey for truth and freedom.

As if in answer to a prayer, in 1966 I was introduced to a radically different way of life. I had the good fortune of living in the San Francisco Bay Area, where I found myself in the middle of a cultural renaissance. Young people from all over the world were converging there, participating in a massive experiment exploring new lifestyles, philosophies, spirituality and experiential approaches to psychology.

Throughout my journey for truth I crossed paths with a number of teachers that broadened my perspective on spirituality as well as psychological modalities that were emerging at that time. In 1969 I was part of a two-year experiment utilizing Fritz Perl's Gestalt Therapy, as well as introduced to Zen meditation by Suzuki Roshi at his Zen Center in San Francisco. I was also a student of Stephen Gaskin, an eclectic spiritual philosopher who exposed me to many of the world's spiritual traditions. I had inadvertently stepped onto the spiritual path, that was to guide the rest of my life.

I wasn't a particularly good student. Despite having excellent teachers, I was undisciplined, self-indulgent and easily distracted. Unlike the people I saw around me I was unable to put a stop to desires and thoughts to stay in the present moment as instructed. I concluded that because of my shortcomings I must be fundamentally flawed. The strategy I evolved to undo these problematic tendencies took me on a twenty-eight-year search from 1968 to 1995 and took precedence over establishing a job, home and family. I lived on a shoestring and was following wherever the search led me. I lived in retreat centers and ashrams, as well spiritual and intentional communities. I travelled to the four corners of the globe and explored a litany of teachings.

I also became a teacher and practiced professionally in most of the disciplines I studied. I took to heart the old adage that if you really want to know something, you should teach it. I taught emotional-release therapies, Eastern spirituality and breathwork. I received my Master's Degree in Transpersonal Psychology, at John F. Kennedy University in California, and at Norwich University in Vermont.

In 1980 I co-founded a growth center in Berkeley, California with Marc Allen (the founder of New World Library), Shakti Gawain (the author of *Creative Visualization*) and Tolly Burkan (the fire-walking teacher to Tony Robbins). In the mid-eighties, I co-taught a month-long hypnotherapy/NLP course at Esalen Institute, as well as worked with Denver General Hospital's cancer support group (where a number of remarkable healings took place with people I worked with). In 1990 I co-founded the Transpersonal Hypnotherapy Institute, that became one of the top institutes in the field of professional hypnotherapy training.

Throughout my journey to find myself, I classified myself as a "wounded healer," and my primary motivation was the search for a "better me." Little did I suspect that my three-decade search would come to an abrupt halt on the other side of the world.

It was September 1996 when I had heard from several friends that had gone to see a teacher in India named Papaji. They shared with me that Papaji had the reputation of "waking people up." I saw dramatic shifts in them in the short time that they spent with him, and I felt a sense of peace and power from them that I had not previously experienced. I was so impressed, that I booked a flight to India.

My awakening with Papaji came out of nowhere, as naturally as if it were an everyday occurrence. It is hard to describe in words, and hopefully as you go through your own Radical Awakening, you will experience these spaces as well. My awakening happened one morning when Papaji was walking into the room where he gave his public meetings. When he walked past me, I looked in his eyes and saw within them a vast, conscious universe. I remember being blown away by what I was seeing, and thinking, "Wow, this vast universe is what he must be connected to all the time!"

Then, in a flash, I was plunged into that vast universe. I felt my identity merge into that universe. The "I" or "me," that had previously been my primary reference point disappeared. I saw myself as an infinitesimally small object, floating in a sea of aware consciousness.

I looked around at my immediate environment. It felt as though there was no one looking, but instead was an aware consciousness witnessing a divine unfolding. I felt as if I was touching into a reality that had always been present but not previously experienced.

From that point on, though I still experienced a full range of emotions such as joy, compassion, anger, fear and hurt, my relationship to them shifted. In the background was an underlying, ever-present calm and conscious space. Even in the most challenging situations this intimate awareness softened what I was experiencing.

This change unfolded, not as a function of my working on myself, but as a result of a fundamental shift in identification from my previous identity to this aware consciousness. Shortly after this happened, Papaji gave me the name "Ramana," after his beloved Master, Sri Ramana Maharshi.

About a week later I asked for Papaji's blessing to give a workshop for the Lucknow community on the Enneagram, an ancient Sufi system of "Self-Remembering." I was surprised when he not only gave me his blessing, but then pointed to a handful of people in the room and said, "You work with Ramana." He suggested that I do the workshop in *Satsang*

Bhavan, where he gave his spiritual talks, rather than at a friend's guest house.

To my amazement, he then told me to conduct the workshop in the very seat he conducted his own meetings. In a later encounter he gave me some instruction on how to do the workshop, where he made sure that his message of *satsang* would be included. *Satsang* is a Sanskrit word: "*sat*" means the truth of who we are as this aware consciousness, and *sang* is short for *sangha*, which means "spiritual family." So *Satsang* is when a spiritual family comes together to celebrate the truth of ourselves as this aware consciousness.

I immediately began to consider how I could best work with the people Papaji had referred to me. From my experience teaching Neuro-Linguistic Programming, a science of how to bring a person into a particular state of consciousness, I decided to use my own new-found consciousness as the model for the state I wanted others to experience. I also pulled from everything I had learned during my years of study of psychology and spirituality.

During the process of developing my work, the name "Radical Awakening" spontaneously came to me. I remember when I first wrote the words down on a piece of paper in my room in Lucknow, how much they resonated with me. Awakening was the perfect word since it points to a sudden shift in identity rather than a progressive path of improving the persona. Before I left India, Papaji said to me, "Be as Ramana." I understood this as his instruction to be the consciousness that Ramana Maharshi is in Truth, as well as to carry his message of Truth to others.

Ramana Maharshi stated, "We are so engrossed with the objects and appearances revealed by the light, we pay no attention to the light itself." Once the light of Awareness is known, problems are recognized as simply reflections of that light. Indeed, everything we perceive exists in this light.

For the last twenty years I have been something of a Johnny Appleseed when it comes to Radical Awakening. I would light a candle of awareness, but the effect was limited because the knowledge was confined to the number of people I could meet personally through my workshops and private sessions. My hope is that this book can light many more candles. Peace, joy, and happiness are our birthright, is our very own true nature. It's my heart-felt prayer that this book awakens you to what you are in Truth: a universe far beyond any limitation or unfulfilled potential, where the soul feels a deep connection with all living beings, and the heart reaches out to embrace that connection experiencing truth and freedom.

With love and blessings,

Ramana

2019, Arunachala, India

INTRODUCTION

Would you be interested in learning a meditation for which you do not need to set aside a special time and place because it is present with you wherever you are? And what if this meditation didn't require effort to stop your thoughts, practice presence or even try to relax? What if this meditation, over time, became integrated into your daily life, offering a peaceful and centered place to go, even in your most stressful and demanding situations? A Radical Awakening offers such a meditation.

The key to this meditation lies in directly experiencing the underlying substance of all existence. The ancient Indian teachings, called the 'Vedas,' describe a state of being that is always present, ever still, and is the unchanging fabric of everything that exists. These teachings call this state of being *pure consciousness*, or *pure awareness*. In India's Goddess culture, they state that this fabric of everything is made up of that *pure love*.

This pure awareness and love is infinite and formless, like space. When the Apollo astronauts viewed the earth from outer space, they were awestruck by a sense of vastness. It stopped their minds. When they became aware of its stillness, they also became still. They were in a state of meditation. In the same way, when you recognize yourself as pure consciousness, you realize you are always in the stillness of meditation.

The ancient teachings also go on to say that pure awareness is our *true nature*, or our *true self*. How can we understand this? It is like intimacy. There are those special times with another where all boundaries disappear, and all that remains is a heart-felt connection. You come to rest in a space where you and the other are one as love. When you merge with pure consciousness there is perfect intimacy. You *are* that consciousness.

Our true self is so close, we tend to look right past it. We seek for it in some other time and place, when it is always already present in the very place we are, in this moment. In 1969, my Zen teacher Suzuki Roshi told me that the awakened state is our *true nature*. I often wondered, "If it is our true nature, why isn't everyone there all the time, or at least part of the time?"

The traditional explanation is that the true self is hidden behind the illusion that we are separate from everything, thus losing our connection with everything. Once this connection is lost, we become lost in our illusion of separateness, sometimes called our *separate sense of self*. Our attention then goes from the resting state of pure consciousness into the stresses of our everyday challenges. Our life then becomes a survival game, managing our feelings, careers and responsibilities. We become obsessed with avoiding pain, and searching for pleasurable experiences as a solution for dealing with life.

In a Radical Awakening, the mind becomes silent, which allows us to hear the resonance of the heart. We reconnect with the intimacy of our true selves, uniting us with all that is. In this unity we see everything, even the challenges in life, as the unfolding of divine perfection. This resonance with the heart then becomes our guide to help us through our life's challenges.

Your Own Personal Guide on your Journey

Imagine being in the privacy of your home with your own personal spiritual guide. Together, you embark upon a journey unlike any you have taken before. You are moving into the depth of yourself, where at each step something new is revealed, and you become more expansive, brilliant, and free.

The book is accompanied by audios that you can download into your computer or mobile device. In the audio recordings I will guide you, step-by-step on your journey. First we will destabilize the structure of the mind that forms repetitive thinking patterns and unwanted habits. Once the structure weakens and finally collapses, you will get a glimpse of your true self as divine consciousness. This glimpse could be so compelling that you begin to identify yourself as this divine consciousness.

After your awakening, sometimes this glimpse becomes lost within the challenges and difficult situations in our lives. The second part of this book is dedicated to helping you find your way home when lost. The tools presented are designed to help you stay in the awakened state, and to deepen your newfound state of awareness. Some tools act as signposts along the journey. You will be able to listen to the meditations over and over until your newfound awareness is stable and becomes second nature.

A Divine Invitation

The invitation is to become who you really are. This invitation is designed to move you beyond your limitations and to break through to the freedom which is your birthright. It's a journey into the depths of your being, where everything you thought you knew is challenged.

In contrast to many conventional techniques used for consciousness expansion, that usually focus on removing the obstacles to awakening, this book starts with awakening first. From the awakened viewpoint, obstacles are seen with insight and inner wisdom. You're shown new possibilities that were previously hidden.

I realize that such claims are suspect to the discriminating reader, and rightly so. The ancient sages wisely stated that the spoken word could not be the ultimate truth, but only a conceptual presentation of it. For this reason, this book is written as a *practical,* step-by-step guide. The approach in this work is *showing*, rather than telling. Your direct experience of your true self leads your journey. In this way, your own *experience* becomes your teacher.

The key to this approach is in its simplicity. All that is required is to shine the light of awareness on the dark areas that keep us from seeing who we really are. Like the objects in a dark room that becomes clear when a light is turned on, the true self is revealed when the light of consciousness illuminates it. Once recognized, this light carries throughout our daily life.

Skeptical? Good! I encourage you *not to believe a word that I say* but instead find out *for yourself* what is true. *My invitation is this:* be like a good scientist and set up an experiment to test the validity of what I say. Let your own experience be your inner guide.

This invitation to you is not a casual one, and I encourage you to consider it carefully. In your journey, you may find you may need to leave all concepts and thoughts about who you are. After a Radical Awakening, our thoughts, with all of its chattering and instructions, become something to observe, rather than something that defines our lives. Life then becomes a mystery to explore, rather than a constant situation to control.

When these techniques are implemented as a practice, this book has the potential to change your life radically. From the awakened perspective, life can be seen as a divine creation ever renewing itself.

I believe that you have picked up this book because you know, and have always known, that there is more to reality than what you've seen or been told. What is missing is not something *else*, nor is it somewhere else. If your heart is moved to take this divine invitation, it will be my privilege and honor to join you on this journey home to your true self.

How to Use this Book

The core of this book is the audio recordings. The written material supports the recordings. This unique format requires you to reorient yourself about how you typically read a book. When you see this symbol:

put down the book and listen to the audio recording. After listening to the recording, go back to where you left off in the book. The place where you left off is marked with this symbol:

It indicates that there is written material to help review what happened for you during the recording. In it I ask you to reflect on specific aspects of your experience, and I explain the working principles behind the exercise. In this way you often have important insights that enliven the experience for you. I also present additional tips if you did not "get the exercise," and I encourage you to go through it again.

Important Note

I cannot overemphasize the importance of not reading past the point where you are directed to listen to an audio recording. To go on reading past the audio symbol 🔊 will leave you ill prepared for what follows. Without the direct experience the audio provides, what you read will only be concepts. This book is carefully crafted to take you step-by-step to your awakening. So, I recommend you follow precisely the system that has been laid out for you.

Step-by-step instructions for using the recordings in this book:

1) Download ALL of the recordings here:

http://tinyurl.com/jjwtqew

    a) The recordings can be downloaded into your computer, Smartphone, tablet or iPod. I recommend you download them in the place where you will have easiest access to them. Most people download them into their phones.

    b) If you have any problems with the audio download, please refer to the Appendix at the end of the book, especially if you are using an iPhone or iPad. In the Appendix there is also an email address to my tech person, Natec, who can answer any question you have.

    c) Organize the recordings and make them easily accessible by putting them in a separate folder.

2) In Chapter Two, when directed to listen to the audio **A Taste of Radical Awakening: The Pen Exercise** leave about forty minutes of undisturbed time to do the exercise as well as the follow-up reading and review.

3) **Important:** There are seven recordings in Chapter Three, *The 7 Steps to Radical Awakening;* each is a step in the Radical Awakening process. Set aside about a half an hour a day for seven days to do each of the steps. After listening to a recording and reading through the review of the recording, try taking what has opened up for you into your life for the rest of the day. Consider the process a seven-day meditation project you invest in your awakening. Feel free to repeat any of the recordings during these seven days.

4) The final recording in Chapter Three is ninety minutes long and combines all 7 Steps into one recording. Listen to this recording after having gone through each step separately, and dedicate at least ninety minutes of undisturbed time to do so. This recording is different than

the recordings of the individual steps, and will give you another way to experience your Radical Awakening.

After that, repeat it as many times as you like. People tell me they find benefit in listening to the recording in an informal setting, like when washing the dishes or taking a walk. With the recording playing in the background, sometimes just a sentence or a phrase brings back the space of awakening. Repeated exposure in any setting, whether formal or informal, will reap rewards. Be creative and have fun with it.

TABLE OF CONTENTS

PART ONE

. . . . ●●●●●●●●●●● . . . .

Your Radical Awakening

CHAPTER 1
What is Radical Awakening?

Consciousness is like air. We dwell in it without perceiving it, or realize that without it we could not survive. – *Ramana Maharshi*

In a *Radical Awakening,* the mind quiets, which allows for the heart to open to a new level of connection with everything. Our actions and decisions are then guided by the heart, rather than the mind. From that point on, every moment becomes an opportunity to surrender to the infinite power of love.

For such a profound change to take place it requires more than just making a decision to improve ourselves. It takes a radical shift in our identity. Ramana Maharshi, one of India's greatest modern saints, proposed that we are *not* the person in the middle of all of our thoughts. He asks the question, if we are not the person in the middle of our thoughts, then who are we? The exploration of this question is at the core of Radical Awakening.

A *Radical Awakening* is not about changing you as a person, improving your character, or solving that character's life problems. Instead, it goes to the *root* of any issue: the mistaken assumption that you are a separate, limited being.

The experience is similar to waking from a dream. When roused from a dream—whether beautiful or frightening—we realize fairly quickly that everything we took seriously in that state was an illusion.

In the moment of awakening, the dream character falls away. The story-line no longer has the same impact that it had in the dream state. Similarly, when we awaken to the true self, we see that the limitations of the character we presumed ourselves to be, has dissolved.

If we consider that our presumed identity is no more real than the character in a dream, doesn't it make more sense to wake up, rather than to work out that character's problems? In place of the dream—the very place you are now, holding this book—there is freedom.

The purpose of this book is to make this awakened state not just something you read about, but rather a living experience that can be endlessly explored. An awakening requires no preparation and is unrelated to any particular religion, philosophy, or doctrine.

You cannot be taught intellectually how to awaken. You can study spiritual concepts, you can read the holy texts of the world's religions, you can practice the most rigorous meditation techniques and you may become well-read, knowledgeable, and even wise by way of these practices. But you can't become enlightened by the power of the mind. Reading words on a page can't reveal your true self beyond the realm of the intellect.

Consider the case of laughter. How could there be a program to teach you how to laugh? Laughter spontaneously arises from an entirely natural place. The same applies to the awakening of Consciousness.

Radical Awakening arises naturally in the recognition of your true self. Moreover, this true self is your default condition. It's not something you need to "get." Not only do you already have this recognition, but you *are* the recognition.

When our point of view shifts, we no longer feel the *need* to constantly experience only higher states of awareness. We find ourselves comfortable just where we are, resting in a state of pure awareness.

The seeker who only looks for pleasurable spiritual experiences is often ill-prepared for the hard stuff life inevitably presents. When the benchmark of our spiritual growth is measured by how many unbroken pleasurable spiritual experiences we may have, the failure to maintain these states is sometimes seen as a personal failure. Even the validity of our spirituality could be questioned.

After an awakening, what is previously seen as a failure is now seen as an even deeper spiritual experience. Challenges are now welcomed as a vehicle to deepen into one's spiritual growth. The awakened awareness can accept and hold two seemingly contradictory states that are happening at the same time: at one level you are aware of life's challenges, and on another level, you are aware of the true self at rest. The confluence of these two levels creates a unique and all-encompassing perspective.

An awakening is more than just an experience of oneness. It's the experience and the radical insight *into* that experience, where you understand: This is not another state, this is my true nature, I am consciousness itself. Without this insight, awakening is not possible; instead, you would succumb to the beauty of the experience and seek to stay there.

An awakening is a shift in perspective that carries into your daily life. In a Radical Awakening, you don't bring yourself into meditation. Instead, when you discover your true self as an infinite, unchanging consciousness, you realize how you as the consciousness is always in meditation. In other words, you are merely hitchhiking a ride on the meditation that is always already taking place.

Once you experience an awakening, it's more difficult for you to fall back asleep into the identity of the dream character. An undeniable certainty about your true nature develops. The Indian masters call this certainty "true knowing," that is always present no matter what difficulties life throws your way.

Ramana Maharshi stated "Consciousness is like air. We dwell in it without perceiving it." For example, if there is a painted backdrop of a peaceful, starry night in an act of a play, you may not notice it because you are only putting your attention on the actors and the story. Even though we do not notice the backdrop of the starry night, it still sets the mood of peace throughout the act. However, when we put our attention *primarily* on the background, the feeling of peace increases. In the same way, when we realize that we are the space of awareness, the peace inherent in pure consciousness can be felt in any situation.

Our true self is like the sun, illuminating and giving life to us and everything around us. Even when clouds obscure the sun, we know the sun is still there. Radical Awakening is like refining our sensitivity to the sun, so we better draw on its life-giving energy no matter what the weather is. We no longer need to depend on sunny days.

In Radical Awakening our perception is refined, and we see through the clouds of illusion. We no longer insist on good times. Whether times are good or bad, we know we are connected with that which sustains us.

Awakening is possible here and now because the Self is far closer than the sun. When we wake from a dream, we find ourselves in the place where we have always been. We are merely lying in our bed; nothing extraordinary has happened. Radical Awakening is a paradox. Though I have described it as best I can, the actual moment of awakening is a mystery. Even I don't know how it happens. Maybe it's like the sunlight on your pillow or a cool morning breeze, and you awake.

Finding the Calm in the Center of a Storm

Meteorologists speak of the 'eye' as the center of the storm, that is so still that even a leaf cannot stir within it. Meteorologists also state that a storm derives all of its force and energy from this calm center. In the same way, the Wisdom Teachings say that the peaceful center of our being, where our true self resides, is a space where all the power and potency in life originates.

The first I had ever heard of this space was in 1969. My Uncle Ed had just returned from his studies with Morihei Ueshiba, the founder of the Japanese martial art, Aikido. Uncle Ed shared with me one of Ueshiba's techniques, called 'soft-eyes,' that Ueshiba credited as the one technique that made him Japan's undefeated swordsman, even to up his death at eighty-nine years old.

One of my Uncle's last memories of Ueshiba was when he was surrounded by seven of his top black belts, and asked them to attack him all at one time. My uncle watched as Ueshiba defeated them with frightening skill. Bodies were flying everywhere, like spokes from the hub of a wheel. Uncle Ed impressed upon me how such a feat is ordinarily impossible, but Ueshiba was master of the transcendental space that "soft eyes" elicited. He recounted Ueshiba's story about how he had discovered this transcendental space:

"I was fasting on water for forty days, and a vision came to me. A purple cloud surrounded me, and everything seemed to be moving in slow motion. Nothing in my vision was distinct. Rather, my attention was on the space that surrounded me, and it felt like there were eyes in my head that saw all around me, including what was behind me. A deep sense of calm enveloped me, and somewhere inside me, I knew I was touching my unchanging, permanent self, soul or essence."

My practice of Aikido with my uncle never elicited such a space, and I shortly lost in interest in the practice.

In 1982 a friend reintroduced me to Aikido. He had joined the San Francisco Ki Society dojo, and he shared with me about his practice of soft eyes. My memory jumped back to the stories of Ueshiba and that magic space. I joined the dojo that week. I was discouraged during my first class because I could not grasp the space of soft eyes. I was told to relax the muscles of my eyes, not to focus on any object in particular, and to widen my peripheral vision and sense what was all around me. I tried but to no avail. I couldn't grasp how someone could sense what is behind them without turning their head around. Then, about a month later, it happened to me. Oddly enough, it was on a tennis court.

I was alone practicing my serve, and soft eyes was the farthest thing from my mind. As I tossed the ball in the air, I suddenly felt that it wasn't me on the court. It felt as if I was outside of myself watching the tennis serve taking place, and yet at the same time, I felt every nuance of my body's movement. There was a distinct sense of timelessness. I sensed the space all around me as if I perceived from different viewpoints simultaneously.

After the toss, the racket hit the ball, and it landed right where I wanted it to, in the far corner of the service box. There was no inner dialogue in my head, like "Wow, that was cool; how did that happen?" My mind was perfectly still. I continued with a series of serves, each hitting the target area perfectly. The ball whizzed over the net, and there was a sense of perfect ease as if everything was happening by itself.

When I entered the dojo that night, I knew the space of soft eyes without a doubt. Our Aikido practice began with an exercise to test our center of balance. In the exercise, someone pushes you, and if you are in your center, you don't fall over. I used to routinely lose my balance and fall backward onto the mat.

This time, a fellow student who was easily fifty pounds heavier than I, gave me a good shove and I did not fall. He tried several more times, and each time I stood my ground. Later during my practice, every exercise was effortlessly executed. At one point my *sensei* (instructor) came over to me and gave me a smiling nod. Usually, I would have been seeking such approval because I never got sensei's attention, but there wasn't a hint of that. My ego that always looked for approval was not present.

Unfortunately, the magical experience of soft eyes only lasted a few days, though there was a sporadic sense of it at times. Eventually, I stopped my practice of Aikido and tennis. I'd become frustrated not being able to find a reliable way to access soft eyes. I even tried to find it in meditation, and again, it only sporadically occurred, without rhyme or reason.

In 1994 when I awakened with Papaji, the magic of soft eyes returned, but in a new way. There were periods when I experienced the intensity and ease I'd had on the tennis court and at the dojo, but more importantly was the ongoing sense of spaciousness, that transformed the quality of my experience. I use soft eyes in Steps One and Two in a Radical Awakening in order to sense the space around us as well as discover the stillness within it.

Practical Benefits of Radical Awakening

There is a common misunderstanding about spiritual life that states of peace and expansiveness have no practical value in everyday life. Is this true? Consider my experience on the tennis court. I was calm, entirely in the moment, without mind or ego. That day was best tennis I had ever played.

Ayrton Senna, three-time Formula One world champion, said that his best driving occurred when there was no sense of himself driving, and everything happened on its own without effort. Senna incorporated meditation into his into his training regime. At first, he was very frustrated by how little he could control his mind. Senna eventually could meditate for hours at a time and experience extended periods with little thinking. He knew that for a race car driver in a sport as dangerous as Formula One, it's a significant advantage being free of random thought and able to concentrate on the task at hand.

Finding your calm center is the key to accessing the resources needed during challenging times. You might ask, "How can calmness lead to action?" Ramana Maharshi gave the example of a spinning top: although it appears still, it's spinning very rapidly, and it's the energy of the spin that keeps the top steady on its axis.

On my yearly pilgrimages to India, I often stopped over in Southern Thailand to fulfill my love of rock climbing. In 2002, while climbing an easy rock face, one I sometimes would even climb without a rope, I took a fall that broke my tibia in several places. I was rushed to a hospital in Bangkok and immediately taken into surgery. A metal plate was put in my lower leg to fasten together the broken pieces of my shinbone.

After the operation, the doctors informed me that I would be in recovery for five days until the swelling went down. Part of this recovery involved being given pain medication several times during both day and night.

I was asked to communicate to the nurse the level of pain I was experiencing by pointing to one of a series of illustrations on a piece of paper that went from a person smiling to someone crying; I always chose the picture of the person smiling. Throughout my recovery, instead of feeling intense contracted pain in the immediate area of the injury, the pain expanded and dispersed out into the space of the room, significantly reducing its intensity.

This dispersion of the pain into a larger space happened naturally with no effort on my part. I knew from my experience of expanded awareness that accompanied my awakening, that the pain was dispersed into the larger space of consciousness. By the end of the incident, my experience of the infinite space of pure consciousness had deepened dramatically. Because of my lack of pain, as well as the fact that my swelling came down in half the anticipated time, I was released in a fraction of the time anticipated.

Love, the Heart and our Divine Qualities of Being

The Sufi *Fourth Way Teaching* refers to an aspect of the true self they call, *essential aspects of being*. Sufi master Faisal Muqaddam, who I studied with for a year in 1982, described the essential aspects of being as "elevated, transcendental versions of the best of human qualities that arise from the heart."

Just as in the Hindu teachings, qualities such as love, compassion, strength and courage are viewed not as part of the ego and personality, but are the expressions of the true self. In my work in Radical Awakening, I call these essential aspects of being our "*Divine Qualities.* These qualities arise from the heart as perfect, loving responses. as the situation demands. For instance, clarity arises in times of confusion, joy when feeling unhappy, or purity when feeling sullied.

After Radical Awakening, essential aspects of being begin to arise naturally. The practice is then to feel, contemplate and reflect upon them. For instance, you may have had a conflict with a friend where you were misunderstood, judged and treated poorly.

You are left with feelings of hurt, bitterness and anger. But because you have cultivated your essential aspects, compassion arises. Rather than treating compassion as a passing emotion, it is recognized as an aspect of your true self. You stay with the feeling and carry it with you as you go through the day.

You may find that the next time you see your friend your response will reflect compassion. Without needing to rehearse the right things to say, a conversation ensues that brings forth understanding and healing on both your parts.

In the early 1990's in my private practice I worked exclusively with survivors of sexual abuse. In many cases, the traumatic events in their lives had left them feeling dirty and used. Working with them was extremely challenging. I remember attending a weekend seminar where the keynote speakers were Ellen Bass and Laura Davis.

At the time, they were the foremost experts in treating survivors of sexual abuse, and their book *Courage to Heal* was the handbook for professionals working in the field. In their opening statement at the conference they emphasized the importance of establishing a new self-image to replace feelings of being permanently sullied.

They spoke in detail about techniques using self-affirmations of being pure and clean, and that through constant repetition the new programming would eventually be accepted. However, they also stated that when the abuse had started at an early age progress was often uphill and mostly unsuccessful. I had not found this to be the case in my work, however.

I developed a course based on my experiences, called Transpersonal Approaches to Working with Survivors of Sexual Abuse. When I opened the course by stating, "Who you really are is pure, and that purity has never been touched," many participants – often survivors themselves – looked at me in confusion and disbelief. I expected that response; it was justified because a verbal affirmation cannot reach beyond the feeling of being sullied when that feeling is imprinted in the core of the personality.

Although this was before my time with Papaji, I was already working with ideas of leading people into an expanded sense of self. During the course I used guided meditation and visualization.

I led the participants into a greatly expanded space in which they were a tiny point in that space. I introduced the light of awareness, which illuminates the space and gives life to everything within it, so that everything is known to be full of life, untouched and pure. Then there was the breakthrough: that the light is their own light and they themselves are pure. The essential aspect of purity arose when their identity shifted from the limitation of the personality and its history, to the light of awareness, which is always pure and without history.

Ramana Maharshi used the word "Heart" as a synonym for pure consciousness. The Sanskrit word is *Hridayam,* which means "this is the center." Radical Awakening is finding your center and honoring the essential aspects of being that emerge from it. It is a life-long journey of transformation, which is illuminated by the light of who you really are. At times, the journey can be difficult and the light is more like a fire which burns away what is false and less than love. The journey starts with awakening, the experience of the true self. This experience can never be forgotten. It is at once the end of the search and the inspiration to go on, ever deeper into the Heart. I am honored to be with you on this journey into the depth of yourself.

Chapter 2
A Taste of Radical Awakening: The Pen Exercise

*O*n 1996, on a warm summer evening in Santa Monica, California, I was about to give a talk on Radical Awakening. I had detailed notes and was prepared to deliver a thorough explanation of Radical Awakening, especially the theory behind it. Suddenly, I recognized that I didn't like the talk at all. Something about the ambience of the evening made me realize that it was too intellectual. I saw myself pontificating, spoiling the beauty of the setting as well as the innocence of the audience. On an impulse I decided to change everything.

The exercise that you are about to hear is what I did instead. I have refined it slightly since then, but the simplicity of it remains the same. It worked well on that evening in Santa Monica, and I hope it works well for you too.

Before you start:

To set up for the exercise, you will need a pen and a comfortable chair. Find a space where you are free from distractions such as cell phones, pets and children. Make sure that you have enough time – about fifteen minutes – to complete the exercise.

Since you will be holding the pen in front of you for several minutes at a time, you may find it easier to rest your elbows on the arms of the chair. You will be holding the pen and looking at it from two positions (illustrated on following page):

Illustration 2-1 Position 1: Sitting in a chair looking at the pen, with head cocked slightly down

Illustration 2-2 Position 2: Head Level, looking over the pen

The audio is enhanced by listening to it through headphones or a pair of earbuds. They not only help block out ambient noise, but they also give you a better sense of my presence, as if I'm there in the room with you.

The exercise will still work fine, however, if you do not have access to headphones or earbuds.

Audio #1 The Pen Exercise

Review:

There may be some readers who found the audio confusing or something of a mystery. If you are one of them, I encourage you to continue and begin the 7 steps of Radical Awakening which follow. In steps two and three there is a much more thorough exploration of the sense of space. You may also repeat the pen exercise if you wish, to see if you can pick up anything you may have missed.

Lastly, I encourage you to take the space of soft-eyes and the expanded sense of awareness into your daily life for a twenty-four-hour period. People have told me that just doing this simple exercise dramatically changed or shifted their experience in different life situations.

CHAPTER 3
Your Radical Awakening

Welcome to your Radical Awakening, where you will be going straight into the heart of Consciousness. It is likely you will experience your Awakening as a natural course of simply being. You cannot intellectually be taught, or be given concepts, of how to awaken. Instead, think of laughter. How could there ever be a program to teach you how to laugh? Doesn't laughter spontaneously arise from a totally natural place? The same is true for your awakening.

This awakening arises naturally in the recognition of your True Self. This True Self is your default condition. It is not something you need to "get to." Rather, it is something that is only revealed through your own direct experience. Throughout this chapter, you will be provided with illustrations to further broaden your understanding of the instructions given in the audio portion of the book.

STEP ONE: OPENING TO THE MAGIC OF SPACE SENSING THE SPACE OF THE ROOM

Radical Awakening is a discovery of our true self. The Self is like a clear sky or starry night, which we fail to notice because we are preoccupied with our thoughts and the world around us. When we look up into a starry night, we become aware of the vast space that holds the stars. I remember how as a youth I liked to lie in the grain fields surrounding my house at night and contemplate space. I sensed how close I was to something beyond me, greater than anything I could imagine. In Step One, we explore the nature of space by using the kinesthetic, or feeling sense. In a Radical Awakening, the sense of space is the doorway to expanded awareness. Once this sense is awakened, we begin to experience the freedom that is inherent within that space. When we transcend the boundaries of the body, it is possible to sense that the space is not just empty air, but filled with our Consciousness

Some instructions for Step One:

You need to do this step in a room that has a window with a view. Before you start, make sure you have read *How to Use this Book* on page , and completed the warm up exercise.

In the audio recording (link below) accompanying Step One, we be exploring both the space of the room as well as the space beyond the room. The following four illustrations will give you a visual sense of the instructions you will be given. The first instruction will be to orient yourself to the four corners of the room in front of you, and then to all eight corners (Illustration 3.1 and 3.2). You will then be asked to sense the entire space of the room (Illustration 3.3), and then the space beyond the room (Illustration 3.4).

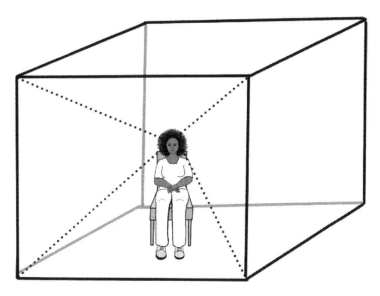

Illustration 3-1 Orienting oneself to the four corners of the room

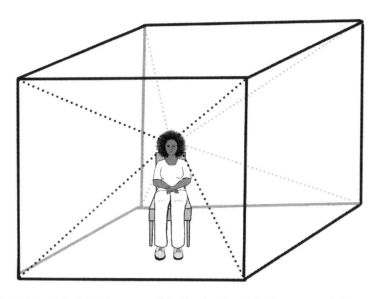

Illustration 3-2 Orienting oneself to the front and back corners of the room

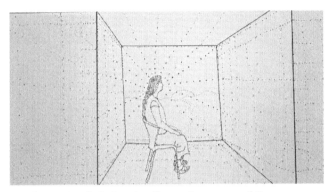

Illustration 3-3 Sensing the entire space of the room

Illustration 3-4 Sensing the space beyond the room

Listen to the audio of Step One

Step One Review

In this review there will be some suggestions offered for you that will help you deepen your understanding of Step One as well as integrate it into your daily life.

Stay with Soft Eyes as Much as Possible

With the eyes closed, you may have found its easier to be in a deeper state. You may have also noticed with your eyes open, there was a subtle, residual feeling of the expanded state that carried over. Yet that subtle feeling is even more powerful than the deeper space since the space can be accessed with our eyes open. By softening our eyes, and staying with the inner experience, we will be able to fully live our daily lives, while still accessing Pure Consciousness.

Create a new habit of noticing the space of consciousness before noticing objects.

You may have discovered in Step One that it takes more effort to put attention on objects than on the presence of the space. An object is defined as anything that is perceived by consciousness, such as a physical object, thought, or feeling. From this perspective, even *people* are perceived as an object to be managed by the mind.

Once we notice an object, the mind creates a story about that object. For example, in passing, someone makes a judgmental comment about you. You brush it off, but notice later you are feeling bad and you don't know why. Without realizing it, a story is created about yourself which is the source of your bad feelings. The construction of a story shows that the mind is regaining its dominance by trying to control the experience. When we focus on the space, however, the story falls away, and there is a sense of ease. Letting go of the story creates an effortless environment.

The trap with thoughts is our unconscious identification with the person in the middle of those thoughts. But what if that wasn't true? What if we were, in fact, the space of consciousness that *perceives* both the objects of thoughts, as well as the accompanying 'me' inside those thoughts? From the perspective of the space of consciousness, it becomes clear that we are *not* the person in the middle of thoughts. This allows us freedom from that, and all thoughts.

Try to avoid the conditioned tendency to look outward at the objects around and within you. A 'softened gaze' assists in maintaining the flow of this new way of seeing by establishing the greater presence of the Self within. Get into the habit, wherever you are, of putting your attention *primarily* on the space of consciousness and *secondarily* on the *objects* you perceive *in* the space.

Listen to Step One again.

Repeating the audio will reinforce the inner sense of stillness. There is no end to how deeply you can go into the stillness, and the more you delve into it, the more stable it becomes. The goal is to bring the stillness into every area of your life, including the ones that are most challenging. This is part of discovering the magic of the space. Now, close your eyes, go within and consider the final question from the audio:

"Is this presence in you? Or, are you in the place it is?"

This question is about discovering an inner knowing, which cannot be put into words. It does not have anything to do with the mind. Perhaps somehow you did know the answer but could not express it in words.

This time, when you are listening to Step One again, trust the stillness and let yourself go deeper into it. Within this stillness you may find a deeper truth, which points to who you really are.

Step Two: Contacting the The Ball Behind the Head Exercise

In Step One, we experienced an expanded sense of self, and discovered that our true selves are not confined to the boundaries of our bodies. In Step Two, we explore the possibility that it is our True Selves are what is seeing through the eyes, and not 'me.' If it were the True Self, known in the Vedas as the "True Perceiver," that has always been the 'seer,' it would mean that not only is True Self that is looking through the eyes, has *always* been looking through the eyes. This can be a startling discovery.

In the movie 'The Matrix,' the protagonist Neo was 'unplugged' from the Matrix. The Matrix was a computer simulated program in which Neo experienced himself as an imaginary character (or in the Vedas calls a 'dream character),' living in an imaginary world he experienced as real. When unplugged from the Matrix, he asked his teacher Morpheus why it hurt his eyes so much to look out them. Morpheus replied, "because you have never looked through them." Once unplugged, he saw for the first time with his real eyes. In the same way, Step Two has the potential of seeing with our 'true eyes."

We start Step Two by placing our awareness behind the head, and in progressive steps, we discover how our *True Selves as Awareness* is who is really seeing through the eyes.

The following drawings illustrate the progression steps that we will be doing in Step Two. You will first be asked to put place a fist behind your head and sense where it is located (Illustration 3-5). Once the location is established, you will imagine that there is an orange floating in this space behind your head (Illustration 3-6).

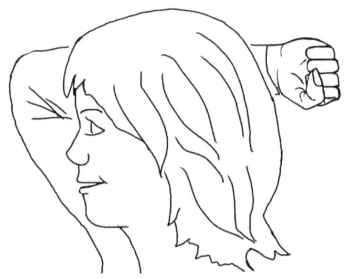

Illustration 3-5 Placing a fist behind the head

Illustration 3-6 Imagining an orange behind the head

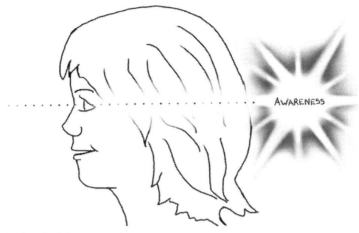

Illustration 3-7 Sensing a luminous awareness behind the heed, that looks through the head and out the eyes.

Important Note: At a certain point in this step you may need to have available a small bottle of pills or vitamins, or a matchbox; either will do. So have one of them nearby when doing the step.

Listen to the audio of Step Two

Review

Why does imagining an orange behind the head give a sense of freedom? To understand this, we need to see how the separate sense of self originated. In this step, we discover how a Radical Awakening undoes the conditioned programing by bringing to light the True Perceiver as Awareness.

In the illustrations below, we see how Awareness, in our infancy, is experienced boundless space. Through conditioning, that sense of boundless Awareness is truncated and experienced as inside the skin, giving rise to the sense, "I am the body."

Below are some illustrations that help explain how we lost our 'oneness' that we all freely experienced as an infant. The first illustration (illustration 3-8) shows a baby enjoying its natural unconditioned state of awareness. Because its primary identification is with the field of awareness, it senses no distinction between itself and the world that surrounds it. It is literally 'one' with its environment. The developmental model of Transpersonal Psychology calls this state, "the pre-personal state," referring to the state that precedes the development of the personality.

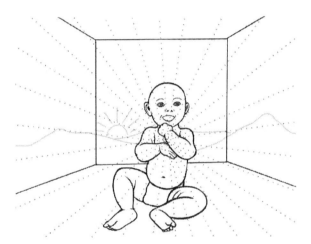

Illustration 3-8 Baby undifferentiated from the space around it

The second illustration, below (*Illustration 3-9*) shows the child's experience after it is conditioned to experience itself a separate. In Transpersonal Psychology, this separation is called 'individuation,' where the child experiences itself as a separate being, with its sense of self is experienced within the boundaries of the skin.

This individuation occurs when the child first perceives Mommy as a separate object from itself. Because the mother seems to be "inside *that* body," the child assumes, "I must be inside *this* body." More so, Mommy is not just some object, but an object the child's survival depends on, and the child instinctually knows this. So at this stage, there is not just separation but also the need to control to this object for its survival.

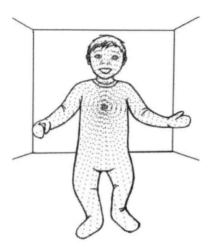

I Illustration 3-9 Awareness is now contained within the confines of the skin, giving rise to the experience, "I am the body."

In Illustration 3-10 (below) Awareness further contracts to a sense of 'me' that is centered in the middle of the head. When the child develops from the pre-verbal state to the verbal state, it is able to put a story as to who it is through a series of continuously rising thoughts. These thoughts give the sense that "who I am is the one in the middle of my thoughts." But you might have noticed in going through the audio in Step Two, your head was empty of thoughts, and that identification with that 'me' inside the head was difficult to identify with. You may have experienced yourself as the Awareness behind the head, looking through the head, and out the eyes, along with a sense of freedom.

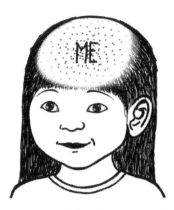

Illustration 3-10: A sense of 'me' now residing in the middle of the head, giving rise to the experience "I not only sense I am in the middle of my thoughts in the head, but this 'me' is who is looking out the eyes. The exploration of this step is consider, through your direct experience of going through the exercise, that it is not 'you' or the 'me' that is looking out the eyes, but Pure Awareness.

One Tip for Continuing to Work with this Step:

If you got the sense that it was Awareness that was looking through the head while going through the audio, test that new way of looking in different by bringing it into different situations in your life for twenty-four hours, or when it occurs to you.

Douglas Harding, a student of Ramana Maharshi, wrote a book called 'Living with No Head,' where he shared what it was like to go through life looking through the empty space which was previously the head.

Step Three Exploring the Scope of Space Experiencing the Infinite Space behind the Body

Step Three, we get a sense of how vast space is. My first attempts at this were not very successful. When I asked people to sense the infinite space around them, the ingrained tendency to look at things naturally led them to look at the walls, floor and ceiling, which limited the space. So, I changed my approach and had them sense the space behind them. I found that people hardly ever do this, and when asked to do so they are caught off-guard, and thus the exercise is fresh and surprisingly doable.

There are a couple of important things to remember as you go through this step. First, it is not important to keep the spine straight; in fact, make sure you use a comfortable chair and sit so that your back conforms easily to it. Second, feel free to use your imagination. In parts of the exercise it is quite okay to picture the vastness of outer space, and this will help the process.

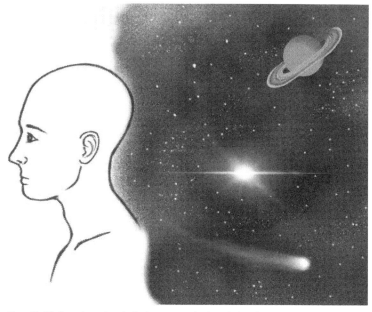

Illustration 3-11 Sensing the infinite space behind the body Okay, so find a comfortable chair and let's begin.

Listen to the audio of Step Three

Review

During the next twenty-four hours, and as you go through your day, try taking a moment to stop and get the sense of the spaciousness that exists behind you. See how it changes the quality of what you are experiencing. Experience what it is like to look in front of you while keeping part of your attention on the spaciousness; even do a common task while staying with this awareness. The more you practice this, the easier and more natural it will become.

This step is especially good for reducing stress. I encourage you to sit down and do it again, even several times throughout the day if you wish. And this time when you listen to it, if you find yourself becoming especially relaxed, then pause the audio and enjoy the space, just groove with it. In doing so, the body learns how to relax, and how to stay calm in stressful situations.

Final Note: There was a point in this exercise when you might have experienced being held by the space behind you. If so, go back now and remember that moment. How much were you thinking? Was there any involvement with the verbal mind? Interesting, right? The mind was largely free of thoughts. And again, as with each step of Radical Awakening, this came about spontaneously, without effort. You were not asked to stop thinking; rather, the mind became free of thoughts because you were experiencing the space that is prior to the mind.

Step Four Exploring the Vastness of Consciousness Looking Out the Eyes

In this step we take our first big leap: we explore infinite consciousness as the seeing through our eyes, hearing through our ears, and feeling through our nervous system.

We explore how the vast, aware, ever-present space we experienced in the previous step is what is actually perceiving the world. If we approach the steps in Radical Awakening as not a set of exercises, but instead seeing it as an unveiling a universe that is usually hidden, you will more easily slip into the Awareness which is always present

In this exercise, we explore how the true seer is always looking through the head and out the eyes – every second of every waking hour. The following illustration shows this perception:

Illustration 3-12 Perceiving awareness looking through the head and out the eyes.

Note: In preparation for this step you need to find an object to look at. The object should have an emotional charge; by this I mean it should make you somewhat uncomfortable and stressed – something like a stack of bills you have to pay, a picture of someone who annoys you, an IRS form and so forth. Have it handy so that at a certain point in the Step you can easily place it in front of you.

Listen to the audio of Step Four

Review

A stressful situation produces thinking. The mind wants to figure out what to do, how to handle the situation. This type of thinking concentrates attention in the head and the "me" becomes very pronounced. We get knotted up with thoughts and the separate sense of self. This is a common problem, and in this step you experienced how it is solved. Again, you were not told to let go of the stress; instead, you experienced a greater dimension of yourself, which is inherently free of stress. Most importantly, you experienced how close this dimension is. This is a key to Radical Awakening: freedom is so close, we only have to be pointed to it. In this case you saw how the true perceiver is here and now, and we miss it because our attention is directed towards identifying with the "me" in the head.

What is the "me" in the head? The natural way of seeing is perceiving awareness, and you experienced how easy it is. In this natural way of perceiving, the mind is not activated, so that our intuition and heart comes to the surface to guide us. Remember when you noticed that the "me" had disappeared, perception took place just fine without it, and there was no worries. This is an important point: we are adding something to our natural state that is obscuring it. In Radical Awakening we remove what is unnecessary so that we experience what is always already present.

as consciousness is formless and still, so too is space. Most important, the deeper we go into space, the more the mind falls away and consciousness reveals itself. Space is a window into consciousness, into our true self.

Step Five The Turnaround Step Awareness Turning Back to See Itself

In the previous step you looked back into the space of awareness behind you. You discovered the natural way of seeing, and that the "me" in the head is something added and is not necessary. So, was it really you in the first place that looked back into the awareness behind you? Maybe that "you" is also unnecessary, and awareness is simply looking back at itself. In Step Five we will dive deeper into the fundamental nature of awareness. We will discover a wonderful truth: while awareness is looking *out* into the world of objects, it is simultaneously looking *back* at itself in its formless state. This step is where the primary identification as "me" shifts to the true perceiver.

At a point in this step you will guided to look into a mirror from the viewpoint of formless awareness as depicted in the illustration below:

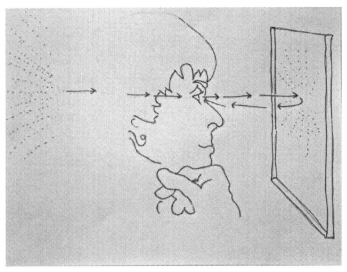

Illustration 3-13 Awareness looks in the mirror and recognizes itself as the true perceiver.

Listen to the audio of Step Five

Review of Step Five

The key moment in Step Five is when Pure Awareness looks back into Its formless infiniteness. Here there is nothing to be seen, since in formlessness there is literally no thing. This moment is subtle and sometimes missed. The mind does not know what to do with nothing, so it just stops. Without thought and mind, there is only the silence and peace of Pure Awareness, and we enter the timeless moment of Now

In the timeless moment, awareness realizes its true nature: that it is never identified with objects, but always and only identified with itself. The silence reveals another truth: that awareness is and always has been the one looking – and not only looking, but hearing, sensing and tasting through the body's sense organs. The body is seen as an instrument) for awareness to experience the world.

Step Five was designed modeling how my awakening happened with my teacher Papaji. I was listening to his words at one of his meetings, as he led my attention back to the True Perceiver. At first, when I looked back nothing was there. I relaxed and returned to the silence. The next time I looked, I was connected with a vast awareness.

When I contacted the vast awareness, I realized that who or what was seeing must be who I am. I understood that the "me" inside my head had not really obstructed awareness, despite what I had experienced otherwise.

In this book I have used the analogy of awakening from a dream, but in that moment I saw that I had never really dreamed, I had never slept. I saw that I had been, and always have been, free.

The moment had a brilliant clarity to it. I saw that even in my worst moments, silent perceiving awareness was present. A tremendous burden was lifted from me. I felt that the story of my past had been rewritten. There was an inner certainty that I am always present as awareness, and this was communicated without words or thinking. It was a communication that occurred not in the mind, but in Consciousness Itself.

Since that time, the knowledge of who I am has never left me. Life still has its ups and downs, and at times I wander into episodes of distraction, discomfort and boredom. I become the fool named Carey (my birth name) again, but not as before. I remember the moment when time stopped, and I become still. I contact again the undercurrent of true knowledge. I like to say I am the fool who can no longer really be fooled.

I sometimes get emails from people after they have done a session with me, even months afterwards. They tell me they suddenly got Step Five and the moment when awareness looked back at itself, even though this part of the step had not been successful for them originally. It was as if a bomb of awakening had been set to go off at a later date.

This was of course good news; it gave me more faith in my work. Yet at another level I realized that whenever a person had an awakening, where Consciousness recognized itself as the True Perceiver, I realized that it was not me, but True Self is reclaiming who we really are. It has its own ways, and I am grateful to be a witness to those ways.

Step Six Ramana Maharshi's Practice of Staying in Pure Awareness

In Step Six, I present Ramana Maharshi's elegant and powerful way to *stay* in the space of consciousness.

Listen to the audio of Step Six

Review of Step Six

Most of the people I see have a common goal of wanting to stay in the peace and heart that Consciousness affords. Step Six enables you to see thought for what it is: an object arising in awareness. It is an exceedingly small object in fact, almost a nothing. Yet, as you have undoubtedly experienced in your life, a thought can have real power. You become annoyed with someone, for example, and then you can't stop thinking about them. You judge them and get angry. There is no ability to listen or to speak rationally; communication falls apart. You blow up at them, or you become estranged and isolated. Perhaps you eventually patch things up, but it is often a long, painful affair. So, what to do in this type of situation?

In the situation I describe there is a strong emotional charge, the chemistry of the body changes, in fact. To attempt to handle the situation at the level of talk is basically fruitless.

Next, reclaim a greater dimension of yourself. Feel your back against the chair, and with each breath sense the space behind you. Find again the feeling that you are being held by space. Now, pick the first thought that comes to you about the person, and see it from the point of view of this space. Don't be concerned about the content of the thought; that is not important. Just see it from the greater point of view, until it is clear that it is a small object in the space of awareness. Watch it and see how it disappears.

Maybe it reappears, so watch it again until it disappears. At this point you will almost certainly be amused by your situation. Sometimes people tell me: "I was just annoyed by a thought!" If you want to go a half step deeper, put your attention on where the thought arises. Become interested in that rather than in thought. Forget thought and remember who you really are.

This process is how you find your center. From this center it is good to straighten out the situation. Radical Awakening has real power in life, but you have to use it. Communicate with the person who annoyed you. Listen with an empty mind, and no agendas. This is calm in th4 center of the storm.

Illustration 3-14 The 'I' thought.

In Step Six we explored the source of this thought. You asked the question: "From where does this 'I' arise?" You were asked to do so without any expectation of what the answer is. Ramana Maharshi emphasized that this question, or what he called "self-enquiry," is not to be answered by the mind. It is left open. It is an invitation to consciousness to reveal the answer.

The "I" thought is like any thought: an object arising in awareness, and like any thought it too has power. It differs from other thoughts in that it is always with us. In any action we perform, in any subjective state we experience, it is present. Sometimes it is exceedingly subtle, more like a feeling, but it is always there. What power does it have? To answer this, consider what it would be like if this "I," this separate sense of self, did not arise, simply did not arise at all. Take the statement: "I have to remember to pick up a bottle of wine for dinner on the way home from work." So, the bottle of wine is picked up on the way home, but there is no sense of a separate self doing it. There is no idea of a "you" doing anything. It just happens. What would this be like?

I was fascinated by the way Papaji worked with people. Over time I noticed a thread that ran through his encounters with people. His timing was always impeccable. He could see when a person was deep enough in the space of awareness to be available for what he wanted them to realize. He was quick to affirm the truth of what was really happening: "*You are this awareness, not a person having an experience of awareness.*" Papaji called this the "tap on the shoulder." In this moment a person awakened to the true self, and in such a powerful way that it was never forgotten.

Step Six stabilizes this realization by seeing how thought is just an object arising in awareness, thus enabling us to stay in awareness rather than becoming lost in identification with thought.

Step Seven The Miracle of Love

What would it like to always be looking from the eyes of the heart? Papaji once said, 'When you look with the eyes of the ego, all you see is ego. And when you look from the heart, all you see is love."

Ancient Indian scriptures state that "the True Self lives in the heart of all living beings as radiant love. This Heart, according to both the Hindu and the Buddhist Tantric traditions, is called the *Anahata chakra* or *heart chakra*. The word *Anahata* represents the aspect of Pure Consciousness from which unconditional love, empathy, selflessness and devotion emerge. It is considered to be an energy center located in the middle of the chest. In this book, I refer to the *Anahata* as the Heart of Consciousness.

In a *Radical Awakening* session, we place our newly awakened Consciousness within the *Anahata chakra*. (Illustration 3-12)

Illustration 3-15 The heart of consciousness.

Listen to the audio of Step Seven

Step Seven Review

Ramana Maharshi refers to this spiritual heart center as, "The Cave of the Heart." He makes the distinction between the physical heart and the Heart of Consciousness. This Cave of the Heart is the energy point that accesses all aspects of our Divine nature. By looking through the eyes of the Heart, Consciousness unfurls into the realization of Pure, Infinite Love.

Despite our experience to the contrary, this life-force blazes in every realm, and in every situation. Even though the mind tries to hide this Divinity, its radiance continues to shine brightly. In the same way that clouds may cover the sun, they never stop the sun's warmth and life-giving energy from radiating. Similarly, when the mind covers up the Love that We Are, that Love continues to emanate its purity and sustenance for all time.

After Papaji's passing, I came to Tiruvannamalai and the mountain Arunachala. I discovered Ramana's love of the mountain. Here is some of what he wrote about Arunachala:

"A bird that rises from the earth and soars into the sky can find no place of rest in midair but must return again to the earth. So indeed must all retrace their path, and when the soul finds the way back to its source, it will sink and be merged in Thee, Oh Arunachala, Thou ocean of bliss."

"Oh Undefiled, abide Thou in my heart so that there may be everlasting joy, Oh Arunachala."

Ramana never held back about Arunachala. Perhaps his favorite description of the mountain, however, is taken from Jnanasambandar, the seventh century Tamil poet-saint, who described Arunachala as "a condensed mass of Pure Consciousness." Here, *Jnana* is the word for

Reality, the Self, Consciousness itself.

Each year I bring a group of people on a three-week retreat to Arunachala. The most common experience they have when looking at Arunachala is that their mind becomes silent, followed by tears of love and connection. These retreats are the most rewarding part of my work because they stabilize peoples' awakening in the silent transmission of the Heart.

There is secret in Step Seven:

We needn't wait for love.

Love is not something that happens in the future.

It is here

because we are here as the Self.

Love is *our* radiance

bringing light to all our "others."

And this love shall shine so bright

that there is only love

dissolving all the seeming differences of the world.

The calm center is not a place you go to; it is in the very place you are. The key to staying in the center is to remember it, remember it as you remember someone who is precious to you, whom you love. When you love, you naturally cultivate the environment of love, which draws you back to the center. Papaji said:

"There is a perpetual fathomless pull of Love into Love, an undercurrent of forever expanding Self into Self.

The more you go into this Fathomlessness the more you will be pulled, attracted, dissolved into It.

This Beauty is attraction and as you go deeper into it you will be more in Love every moment.

Love doesn't ever disappear, as you always are its pureness.

Once you fall in love with your own Self, there is no escape from it."

In India there is a story about a farmer who, while tilling his field, finds the world's largest diamond. In his ignorance, he does not recognize what it is and considers it a big pretty rock. He takes a piece of rope and ties the diamond around his cow's neck and resumes tilling the field. A diamond merchant who happens to be passing by notices the farmer and realizes that he doesn't know the treasure he possesses. He approaches the farmer and offers him a sum of money for it, enough to buy three cows. The farmer thinks, "This man is a fool," and gladly accepts the money. If instead the farmer had realized what he'd found, he and all his future generations would have been saved from poverty.

In Radical Awakening you experience something precious. Remember it and that it is not just another experience. Honor what you know is true, which after all is who you really are. Remember Radical Awakening for what it is and you will be rewarded beyond measure.

It took me a while to recognize the diamond Papaji gave me. At a certain point, I realized without a doubt what my life is about: to honor what I was given by my Master, to live my life so as to always receive his gift. In this way, I have to thank you the reader most of all, because the Seven Steps and the time I spent creating them have been the best way I could have honored his gift.

PART TWO

· · · · · · · · · · · ● ● ● ● ● ● ● · · · · · · · · ·

Living the Awakened Life

CHAPTER 4
At Life's Crossroads: Choosing the Path of the Heart

One of my most profound insights with Papaji occurred in *satsang* when he addressed the question of how to *stay* awake once awakened. He placed his right hand in front of him with his index and middle fingers, forming a "V" shape.

He then took the index finger of his other hand and pointed to the juncture where the two fingers met. He said, "Here is the point where we are at any given time, at a crossroads of choice. If we go down this path (as he traced the length of his index finger of his right hand), we can choose the heart. If we go down this path [tracing his middle finger] we can choose the mind.

Life presents this choice every waking moment of our lives." To emphasize that the choice is in fact ours, he said," Your power to choose the path of love is like the power of a king over his dominion."

Illustration 4-1 Path of the heart and path of the mind

My first reaction to this was one of disbelief. I had never experienced these things as a matter of choice. The mind had seemed to arise automatically and I was caught in the middle of it with no idea how I got there. I thought about this for some time.

I remembered Papaji saying at a previous *satsang* that the only thing more powerful than the mind is the heart. During my awakening, when I directly experienced myself as consciousness, I had seen how consciousness is prior to the mind. It is the space where the heart reveals itself. I began to understand that my awakening did give me the ability to choose the heart.

Over the following years I explored the choice Papaji spoke of. The process was something like the way a baby learns to walk. I would struggle to my feet, and then stumble and find myself sitting on my butt again. It astounded me how ingrained the point of view of the mind was.

At times I would go through several days where literally every decision came from the mind, and I would only recognize in retrospect that this had been the case. What kept me going was faith in Papaji's words and my firm intention to reclaim the dominion he said was our birthright. I was aided by life itself, during those critical times where it was obvious, I had to pay attention or suffer real consequences.

After each crossroads where I had chosen the path of the heart, I noticed that something in me was waking up. It was as if I had a new muscle and it was getting stronger. I became increasingly aware of life's crossroads, even many small ones I would have usually dismissed or been unconscious of.

It took several years of bringing my awareness to each of these crossroads and choosing the heart, before this new way became easy. At a certain point, I noticed I was naturally drawn to the path of the heart, as if love was choosing itself.

The heart is our natural condition. The persistence of the mind keeps us from experiencing this. Thoughts occupy much of the space of consciousness. Thoughts and feelings are inextricably tied together, and when we are stressed, they feed off of each other and overwhelm us. We go into the fight or flight mode, and the mind becomes even more dominant. It seeks frantically for answers to solve the problem, and this pushes us even further into the mind. When this happens, discovering the way of the heart seems impossible.

In overwhelm, the nervous system is like a pressure cooker, where thoughts and feelings become compressed into the space of the body. Opening to the magic of space is like hitting the release valve, so that they can disperse relieving the pressure. As you have already experienced in Radical Awakening, once space opens, the heart can reveal itself. From there, it becomes easier to choose the path of the heart.

In the following I present some important crossroads you may encounter on your journey of awakening, as well as pointers to help you choose the right path. Also included is a *sadhana* (spiritual awareness exercise) that will help you stay in your center while doing so.

These crossroads are not arranged in a particular order, and you may not encounter all of them; everyone's journey is unique. I hope the pointers act as signposts and better enable you to choose the path of the heart.

Crossroads One: Major Life Change

When a person comes to the crossroads of a major life change, it usually involves their job, their living situation or a primary relationship. Sometimes all three are present since they are often closely related.

There are also other major changes that can occur such as a health crisis, death of a loved one or chronic depression. Times of major change are particularly challenging because they can affect basic security, more than just the usual challenges to our self-image and ego. Wrong choices in these situations can have real consequences. In light of this, it is vital to find your center and follow your heart.

"Jenny"

Jenny, a bright woman in her thirties, was going through three major life changes. Her husband had just left her, she had little money of her own, and she and her two young sons had moved in with her mother.

The divorce looked like it was going to be long and messy, and she was scared, frozen and unsure what to do. Livelihood was her first concern. Before getting married she'd had a successful career as a graphic artist, but she had not worked in over seven years.

In her Radical Awakening session, she opened beautifully to the magic of space. She was no longer overwhelmed by her thoughts and feelings, and she was amazed that this was even possible.

She left the session with a more expansive sense of self and a feeling that somehow things were going to work out. I gave her a daily assignment to choose one of the 7 Steps recordings and listen to it each morning before she started her day. She agreed and told me she was looking forward to doing so. We scheduled our next session via Skype to take place in three weeks.

At that next session she told me that the previous three weeks had been difficult for her, but she'd found a place in her heart to go to when things got bad. She shared how the morning meditation helped her find that place, how with each listening she returned to the expanded sense of space and the heart. She was no longer frozen in fear and was handling things one step at a time.

She told me how the anger towards her husband had begun to change, which she attributed to working with the audio of Step 7. Before communicating with him, she listened to the train platform scene and actually used her husband as the person she was meeting.

Each time she listened to the recording, she got in touch with the love that had first brought them together. More than that, when she allowed her heart to expand further, she saw how love is always present and does not depend on relationships; instead, relationships are transformed by love. After that, her conversations with her husband worked out far better than before.

At our last meeting, about four months after her initial Radical

Awakening session, she told me she was studying to re-enter the graphic arts field and she felt confident she would succeed. She said that when she had chosen the heart instead of the mind, although it was sometimes scary, things somehow worked out in a remarkable way she had not anticipated.

After seeing this occur several times she developed more faith in continuing to choose the way of the heart. She also discovered that by contacting the magic of space, her thinking became less cluttered and clearer, enabling her to make better decisions.

At the close of our time together, although she still had challenges to face, she knew that there was a calm in the storm where she could go, and this gave her new hope. She also said that she saw the grace behind her challenges and how they brought her to new awareness and understanding. She thanked me for the inner peace that was opening in her life and especially for the change she saw in her children because of that peace.

Crossroads Two: Impatience and Judgment

One of the keys to not getting caught in judgment, both of others and ourselves, is to identify its presence before it has a chance to grab hold of us. This can be tricky since in its early stage judgment is largely hidden. To examine our judgments also requires an honest look at ourselves, and this can challenge some of our most sacred beliefs.

But if we are willing to look, we can discriminate between what is real and what is a distortion. Once we recognize the distortion, judgment becomes unstable; it falls away and a new space opens, allowing for the path of the heart to be a clear choice.

Judgment progresses in stages. It is barely visible at the earliest stage and seems relatively harmless. In later stages, although we notice it, it already has a grip on us and we become increasingly powerless in the face of it. In this section I present the four stages of judgment, and outline some of the traps we can fall into if we are not paying attention.

The First Stage of Judgment

In the first stage, judgment is almost invisible as it weaves throughout the fabric of our lives. Every day we make decisions about what is good or bad, right or wrong, without inspecting if judgment is present. Our mind tells us that we aren't judging anything, only making decisions. It all seems innocent enough. But what if some of the apparent decisions contain an emotional charge? The difference between a decision and a judgment is that a judgment carries with it an emotional charge. Although it can remain hidden, the emotional charge does not lie dormant. Since we frequently return to the same judgment, the charge gets reactivated and grows, like a seed planted in fertile soil.

The Second Stage of Judgment

In the second stage, we become plagued by what seems to be a growing amount of annoying situations and people in our lives, and we find ourselves short on patience. But what is the source of this impatience? Could it be that it stems from the frustration we experience when we can't control a situation and the people we are encountering?

For instance, have you ever found yourself waiting at the end of a long bank line and asking, "Why don't the people who run this bank bring out more tellers?" You notice a customer who is taking an inordinate amount of a teller's time as she rifles through a stack of his papers and ask yourself, "How can someone be so inconsiderate as to bring that much paperwork on a Friday afternoon when the lines are the worst?"

Then, when it is finally your turn to approach a teller, she closes her window in front of you. Now you're pissed and blame it on the bank's lack of caring about their customers. You start fuming about the bank's indifference and your lost time. Sound familiar?

Or maybe you are irked by someone's behavior, and each time it happens, you become more irked. It could be a friend who only talks about himself or someone who has a habit of always being late. It is easy to take this personally and believe you're being slighted.

It is important to understand how impatience is tied to judgment. Perhaps your impatience in the bank line had more to do with your judgment than the actual time "lost" waiting in line. Or perhaps the real reason for your annoyance with your friend is not their behavior, but your judgment about it and about their character. If you can see impatience as the signal that judgment is present, it will help halt the judgment's escalation.

"Martha"

Sometimes the second stage of judgment turns into self-judgment, and this can be devastating. A fifty-year-old osteopath, Martha, shared with me how she could no longer trust herself, citing a long string of unsuccessful relationships. She spoke of how she always made bad choices with men.

I listened to her stories, which ended with her conclusion that something must be seriously wrong with her. She started crying and looked at me with tears streaming. "Sometimes," she confessed with a hint of fear in her eyes, "I feel so stuck and hopeless that I get afraid I'll never get out of it."

I asked her to look at who or what was delivering the self-judgment. She quickly replied, "They are horrible voices, which leave me feeling horrible about myself, and the more I try to stop them the more they come back at me!" She paused for a moment, and in a change of tone, said, "And that's when the hopelessness comes in."

I could see that Martha's thoughts were imploding within her, so I asked her to begin to open to the space of awareness. My biofeedback readings showed an almost immediate release.

She said she felt her heart beginning to open. I invited her to be brave and choose the path of love. She agreed. I then asked her to go to one of the voices that plagued her and open her heart and embrace it and try to hear and feel what the voice really wanted.

Martha was silent for several minutes, and a tear trickled down her cheek. She said in a quiet voice, as if speaking to a deep part of herself, "Love. It wants love; they *all* want love." I didn't have to give any further guidance; my biofeedback readings indicated a complete release.

In my next session with Martha I asked her a pointed question: "What is being protected by making bad choices with men?" It took her a while to admit that she'd never trusted her father, who throughout her life had never really been present, and that their relationship had been a series of one disappointment after another. She said that, contrary to how it seemed at first, in the end the men she chose turned out to be like her father, just another disappointment.

I asked her to continue looking at who or what was being protected, to go deeper.

After some time, she exclaimed, "I am not protecting anything! I am choosing relationships with men like my father as a way of having another chance to heal my relationship with him."

I asked her with a smile, "And how is that going?" We both had a laugh.

I asked Martha to look again at who or what was being protected, but this time from the ball of awareness behind the head. From that perspective, she said she could see the working of the mind, as if it were all operating in front of her, like a machine.

I asked her to look at what the machinery was hiding. She took some time to look deeper. She took a deep breath and said, "There is a massive judgment about my father that everything in my world validates, that he is the most horrible of all people, so heartless and cold. And not only him, but all men, they are all the worst!"

"Yes," I said, "you are judging your father and also other men. You can know this from your language. You said, 'most horrible' and 'the worst.' These are categorical statements, and categorical statements about others are always untrue, and they are always judgments. Let me ask you, "Is your father really the worst?"

"No, he gave me a roof over my head and put food on the table."

"Was he heartless and cold?"

"It sure felt like it at times."

"But what about other times? Really, look at the years you spent with him growing up."

"Yes, there were times he was kind to me. I can see his clumsiness, like he didn't quite know how to do it, but he tried in his own way."

"And these men you call "the worst;" they weren't that at all. I mean, was one of them a Ted Bundy or an Adolph Eichmann?"

"No, they weren't. There were good times. They were also kind to me, even loving. I was waiting to find their faults. The first time they did something like my father would do, my mind was on them like a bear trap. They turned out to be losers in the end, but I didn't help."

"They were losers?

"No..."

Martha unexpectedly started crying profusely. My biofeedback indicated a loss, the kind of reading people have when they lose a loved one. I asked her what she was feeling so sad about. She looked up at me suddenly from her tears, as if I'd hit the nail on the head, and said, "All the lost years of my life, and all the missed opportunities for a relationship. I have missed out on most of my life. I am the loser."

"Martha," I said, "be careful with your language. Have you really missed out on most of your life? Just examine a typical day. Nine hours of work, eight hours of sleep, some time with yourself, time with friends, and time with your intimate. So maybe the time with your intimate wasn't all roses, but you had a life, didn't you?"

"Yes, I did."

"And there was this other thing going on: judgment. Let me see if I can get to the point: The first spare moment you had, and bingo, there it was. Not just there it was, but if it wasn't there you would choose it, right?"

"I was like an alcoholic, just waiting for the first drink. And once I took the drink I couldn't stop, and it went from judging others to judging myself."

not a loser. You wouldn't be here if you were. Maybe ᵢe sobriety."

ght. And the first thing I have to do is stay out of bars. ancel my subscription to match.com and dedicate time to being ᵤ r a while."

"Excellent. Do that and let's see the change that happens as a result."

In our next session, when I like to see a person again a year later to catch up on what is going on in their lives, Martha told me that she'd met a man in her tango class. At first, she didn't feel much chemistry with him, but he treated her with respect and courtesy. She admitted that being treated this way made her a little uncomfortable but she was starting to see that being appreciated has its roots in love.

I asked Martha about her father, and she told me she had saved her biggest breakthrough for last. She said her father had recently been in the hospital with pneumonia, and it looked like things could take a turn for the worst. She had spent days with him at the hospital, and she found her judgments of him very petty. At one point, she asked for his forgiveness for judging him so harshly. She then shared how she'd found a deeper level of what was being hidden by judgment. She discovered that underneath the hurt and disappointment was a little girl who just wanted her daddy's love. She further shared how feeling vulnerable was not so scary anymore but sometimes was empowering. She went to her father and told him that she loved him, and that the little girl had always loved him.

Her father told her that he had always loved that little girl, and how it pained him to see her go away. He apologized for not being able to do better. He had not known what to do except harden his heart to cover the pain. She told me how they held each other and wept together.

The Third Stage of Judgment

In the third stage, judgment becomes a primary pattern in life. Yet often it is still not recognized as judgment; instead it feels like common sense: we are just taking care of ourselves and watching out for others. It then becomes our 'job' to police the wrong-doings of the people around us.

Judgment is well hidden in this stage. Instead of openly letting people know of our judgements, and freely speak badly about the 'offender' to others. Although sometimes it seems that our current culture thrives on gossiping about others, in this stage gossiping and undermining a person's character in some way weaves it way into the majority of conversations. An air of righteousness develops, as undermining the people who you are judging is seen as a noble job.

Close alliances are formed between you and the one being 'wronged,' as you now both have a common enemy. This behavior ranges from seemingly just having a fun gossip session to lines being drawn between those you feel safe with, and others who are potentially dangerous. Any thought that we may be part of the problem is not considered. We feel justified to bring justice to the 'wronged.' Criticism, judgement and finding fault in another, or others, becomes an unconscious obsession.

There is a well portrayed spoof of this stage of judgment in an episode of the HBO series *Curb Your Enthusiasm* called "Palestinian Chicken." In the episode we find that Sammy, a teenage girl not above blackmail if it serves her, harshly judges her mother loudly smacking her lips and exclaiming "ah" after every drink.

Embarrassed by her mother's actions, she's convinced that everyone else is equally embarrassed and feels that she has to put a stop to that behavior in order to save herself and everyone else from discomfort. In this episode we also find that Ron, who can no longer tolerate his wife saying "LOL" at the end of a sentences she is speaking. He tells himself that *everyone* knows one should not use LOL outside texting, and feels publicly humiliated every time his wife says it.

Sammy and Ron coerce their friends into a strategy to shame their 'perpetrators' by threatening them to expose the secrets of their friends own wrong doings against the people that they committed to the people in their lives. They have this leverage against their friends because everyone is talking behind everyone else's backs, and involved in their own hidden games.

In the end, everyone's secret affairs, blackmail and backstabbing is exposed, ending in total havoc, but done in a way that is totally hilarious.

We laugh, because we know that what is being poked at is our own human weakness to judge, gossip, and unconsciously backstab even the closest people in our lives.[1]

The Fourth Stage of Judgment

In the fourth stage of judgement, where it cannot be hidden to yourself or others. Actions at this stage are oftentimes openly hurtful, even vicious. It is here we discover that primal wounds, hurt and fear often underlie our judgments. These are projected out onto the people we judge, who appear dangerous. The body-mind's protection system goes on high alert, and we can be driven to do things we later deeply regret.

Without self-inspection, judgment is not recognized as judgment, in any of its stages, It is dismissed as unimportant, reasonable or somehow justified. This inspection calls for a certain courage, an unflinching determination to get to the bottom of our actions. This can be difficult, but in my experience, it is the only way to break through to the freedom we long for.

"Jack"

Jack was a forty-two-year-old professional who had attended one of my lectures and then scheduled a Radical Awakening session with me. In his session, he said he had done a good deal of work on himself over the years, including many different approaches to therapy and spiritual practices.

Jack said that he came to the private session to gain greater understanding and insight how, after all of the personal work he had done, he could have acted out with such in such a hurtful way at the time of his breakup with his wife Adele. He said, "it was like a person I never knew

1. This episode won the Directors Guild of America award for Outstanding Directorial Achievement in a Comedy Series. It is my favorite episode in the whole series, just because it can be so darn funny and still contain a powerful message. Note: the series is written for adults, not children, so view with discretion. Here is a link to watch Curb Your Enthusiam, "Palestinian Chicken": https://www.amazon.com/The-Divorce/dp/B0088W9OW2

jumped out of the shadows like an angry animal pouncing on its prey. Yet she was someone I loved dearly."

Jack thought for a moment. "The interesting thing was more upset about the *way* that the breakup was done rather than the breakup itself." He said that he Adele about the had been having problems for years, and I know she was waiting for me to pull my act together.

He said that his ex-wife, Adele, were in a local coffee shop they often frequented, when Adele opened the conversation by stating firmly, "New Year's is coming up next week, and I thought we could start the New Year with a clean slate by no longer being together." Jack said the statement left him thunderstruck. He had choked back the words – "Ah ... do you think we can talk about this?" – because he knew talking about it was not a real option. All he could say was: "Why?"

Her response was, "Because I can't do this anymore."

Jack said he felt betrayed and angry because of her answer and thought, "*This* is what I get after twelve years of marriage; a line from a bad teenage romance movie?"

Repeating Jacks' words, I said, "So you felt betrayed. What was the betrayal?"

He thought for a while and said with a bowed head, "I guess I thought our marriage was worth more than that; that it was worth more than just giving up and throwing it away. I thought she'd promised she would never do that. The biggest thing was that I felt that we would always have a heart-to-heart discussion, and not have the break-up just come as an announcement with no further discussion."

I asked Jack how communication, in general, was with Adele.

He replied, "Adele really did not like talking in depth about things, and wasn't really good at opening communicating her feelings. As far as I know, she was never in a personal therapy session. Instead, she liked coming to what she called an 'understanding,' about agreements, and then felt that it was on each of us to keep them.

Of course, I agreed with that, but it was done in a vacuum, with no real chance to share the challenges when things were heading toward any breakdown in our agreements, or any chance to renegotiate them. Throughout the marriage I was complicit in this breakdown in communication, not really demanding a deeper look at the dynamics of our marriage, which were many. Maybe because it was the easy way out for me, rather than doing the work to give her a safe place to share her feelings, I let things slide."

"So", I said, "let me make two statements, and you tell me which is truer: Adelle isn't good at expressing her feelings, or Adelle is straight about where she stands in a situation."

Jack paused and swallowed. "She is just straight with things. She let me know that from the first time we were together."

"And you went along with it but also thought it was somehow not okay?"

"Yes, with doing all of the work on myself, I figured that I could do the personal work for both of us.

"Okay, let me try another statement, and see how true it is for you: You judged Adelle."

"I don't think so." Jack reflected for a moment. Well, I did think that I was better than her with the communication thing. Maybe I saw her as not up to the task and not capable of seeing things other than pie-in-the sky relationships, like a fantasy of Prince Charming and Cinderella, hmm. Oh God, I am so busted. I guess I did judge her, but I did not see it!

"Take it easy, Jack. No one is putting handcuffs on you. Be kind to yourself. I often tell people that the worst that ever happens is people make mistakes. You strike me as a guy who can tolerate mistakes."

"Yes, I have been told by others that I am non-reactive to stuff that would drive them crazy."

"So, be that way with yourself, okay?"

"I'll try, but it's going to be hard when we get to our big blow-up."

"Let's get to that now. Tell me about it."

"Adele gave me a month to leave the house. She asked if we could come to an understanding that her decision was for the best. I reluctantly agreed, and we both agreed to be pleasant and to act as adults with each other. Throughout the ensuing month we never broached the subject of our marriage.

To keep my agreement, I promised myself that during that month, I would keep my feelings of betrayal in check. We talked about how it would be nice to continue to see each other as friends after our breakup. She even made inquiries for me to stay nearby in the home of one of our mutual friends. Given the circumstances, things seemed to be working out smoothly."

Jack was quiet for a few moments, and I saw tension enter his face. I asked him what was going on. He said, "A lot."

"It felt like the lid that held back all my stored anger and betrayal just popped off. I fell into my past wounds of abandonment and desertion, which were triggered by my mother and sister's betrayals in early childhood, which were extreme."

"I became obsessed with needing to tell Adelle everything I saw and felt. I felt the weight of the years of not communicating in the marriage and I irrationally blamed her for it. A couple of times during that month, I made an attempt to finally talk, but unfortunately my communication was contaminated with the pent-up emotions I promised myself I would not express. I exclaimed to her, 'We never talk, we never have talked, and why not, in the end, don't we finally get around to it?' I looked at her reaction and realized I had just dumped a load of emotion on her, and said to myself, 'Crap.'

"Towards the end of the month things came to a head for me, and on a fateful evening that would change our future relationship forever, I told myself, 'I have to do this; it is my last chance to have the talk we never had in our relationship. She has no idea what I am going through, and there are things she needs to know about herself, for her *own good*.

"We were having one of our typical quiet Thursday nights together. At least that's what I thought. Adele was reading in her room, and I was in my office trying unsuccessfully to process everything that was coming up for me. The office door was open, and when I saw her walk past the door,

I jumped out of my chair while telling myself, 'Now I am going to do it!'

"I approached her in the hallway and started letting her know everything I thought, saw and felt. I told her how I saw a cold, steel wall go down around the people in her past close relationships when she left them, and how she would cavalierly say, 'When I turn a corner, I do not look back.' I told her how that scared me and I never expected it would happen to me. When that steel wall went down, and she became a person that I sometimes saw, but feared.

"She was so stunned, she did not know what to do with herself. I looked at her shock and felt I was finally getting through to her after all these years, not noticing that I was not pointing out behavior, but attacking her character. After I told her that part of her personality was 'heartless,' she paced around the house not knowing what to do with herself, then went into the bedroom, picked up her purse and coat and walked out the door.

"I stopped and realized that I'd really blown it. Our planned friendship, where we talked about our getting together for lunches and occasionally going out for dinner, was no longer even a distant possibility. I knew that when she walked out the door that night, she was walking out of my life forever.

"What happened after the breakup of your marriage?"

"I went into a serious tailspin. I fell deeper and deeper into the feeling of worthlessness. All types of crap came up for me, mostly about my family and my early childhood. Despite the years of working on myself, with a lot of this material I thought I had worked through, I was shocked to see my behavior, as if all those years of personal work amounted to nothing."

"You mentioned that earlier, when recounting the crisis with Adelle. It is something I sometimes find when a person harbors judgment about another to the point it explodes and when the explosion is out of character for them. There is a good deal of early history pushing the explosion. We should go into that. But I want you to know we won't be taking the 'grand tour,' so to speak. Just tell me about a situation or two that comes to mind about your family."

Jack recounted the following: "My mother would go into these horrible tirades, and one in particular was memorable. I don't remember the circumstances that set this episode off, but I remember how angry she was with my father. While screaming at the top of her lungs, she took all the dishes and cups from the kitchen cabinet and smashed them one by one onto the floor. After she'd emptied the cabinet, her mood shifted into a kind of emotionally comatose state, where she became silent with a blank look in her eyes. She went into the living room, picked up a potted plant, looked at my father and nonchalantly tossed it onto the floor. Then, like a zombie, she placed a chair facing a corner of the living room and sat silently in it staring at that corner for hours.

Jack spoke of another incident, when his mother went crazy and carried him to a small, dark shed locked me in there for "what seemed like an eternity." He said he remember thinking, 'I can never trust her, or anyone ever again, no way; it is just too scary.'"

Jack said that decision unconsciously carried over to every relationship he'd had in his life. "My partners never stood a chance with me. Either I judged that they were not good for me, or I would behave in such an offensive way that I was impossible to stay with. With my wife, I now see that I unconsciously sabotaged my business so she would never get what both she and I dreamed of: to have a life full of fun and adventure in far-away lands."

I then said, Jack, I want you to look at your language."

"What do you mean, my language?"

I explained to Jack, as I had with Martha, how superlatives and categorical statements about others are untrue and always judgments. He said he understood.

I began with: "You say your partners never stood a chance with you. What's the problem with the language?"

"The word 'never;' it's categorical. So, it's not true and it's a judgment, right?

"Yes, and who are you judging?"

"I am judging myself."

"Exactly."

"You say you were impossible to stay with."

"The word 'impossible.' It's the same thing. I am judging myself."

"You say you unconsciously sabotaged your business so your wife would never get what she dreamed of."

"I'm having trouble with this one. It has the word 'never,' so I know it is not true and I am judging, but that doesn't seem to be the whole truth."

"Look at the first part, there are two key words."

"'Unconsciously sabotaged'?"

"Yes. Sabotaged is a 'gotcha' word, something you'd find on Fox News designed to buttonhole a public figure and tar him as an enemy. You never sabotaged anything, and you're not an enemy. What about 'unconsciously?' What is the problem with it?"

"I'm not sure there is a problem. I use that word in my talks."

"Let me make a guess: it is an important word in every modality you've studied."

"Yes it is, but so what?"

"Because it is too easy, Jack We know you didn't sabotage anything, but when you add 'unconsciously' to 'sabotage' then it is easy to make your story true. You can make just about any story true if it happened unconsciously.

In NLP, one of their basic tenants is that we are always making the best choices we can, given the limited resources that we have in the moment." The tenant goes on to say that no one, except maybe a psychopath, deliberately makes a bad choice. The choices, in their limited viewpoint of protection and survival, often make a choice that comes from the only limited options.

"Ramana, said Jack, I see why you warned me about staying honest, because this is making me very uncomfortable. So why did I blow up that night with Adelle?"

"Look at what you were doing at that time," I replied. You were judging her. She had to know everything you were going through, the weight of the years of not communicating in the marriage. You blamed her for that. She needed to know about herself, for her own good. You saw the cold, steel wall go down around people in her past relationships when she left them.

"Whew... okay, I get it."

"Let's make sure. I am going to make two statements and you tell me which is truer: Judging Adelle made you temporarily insane, or your early life history pushed you to the brink."

"The first one; it's not even a close call."

"There are a couple of signposts that can help you if you ever come to that crossroads again."

"There are?"

"You went back on your promise. You gave your word to Adelle and to yourself, and you were going to break that promise. That's a big signpost. I mean, what do you think when a person breaks an important promise to you?"

"There's no excuse, and I lose respect for them."

"Okay, so hold yourself to the same standard. The most important signpost happened at the end: you became willing to hurt Adelle. When you said to yourself, 'Now I am going to do it!' – it was all there in front of you, wasn't it?"

"No, it wasn't. I didn't intend to hurt her."

"But it was going to happen. The key words are *for her own good.* This is when judgment has become righteous superiority, and when you let that loose then someone is going to get hurt."

"I can see what you are saying. I am surprised I didn't see it before. I take a good deal of interest in politics and vote in every election. When a candidate uses inflammatory judgmental rhetoric, what you call righteous superiority, that is a big disqualifier for me."

"It's the stuff that can cause wars."

"I went right to the edge, and then I crossed over the edge."

"You made a moral choice, the wrong one. This is a problem I occasionally find with people who have a lot of experience exploring their history with different therapies: they become fluent with their subjectivity, with their feelings and their supposed origins, but in the process, they become crippled in understanding how the other feels. Their subjectivity overwhelms objectivity and they can let loose on the other in a hurtful way."

"Man, I feel like my life, my whole strategy, is right in front of me. This is knocking the wind out of me."

"You are doing fine, Jack. You have hung in every moment and paid attention and honored your commitment to be honest. The basic idea is to relax and come to an intelligent assessment of yourself. I want you to do this, but not at first with such a highly charged incident as what happened with Adelle. Let's try instead your problems with your business. I don't need to know the details, just what the general problem was. Take your time."

After some time, Jack said, "My attention was scattered all over the place. I loved to divert myself on Facebook and all the minutiae of what was happening with my friends. I like minutiae in general. I would handle every detail surrounding my business, but never get to the nut of the thing."

Our time was up for the session, and I felt Jack had plenty to process. I suggested another session, where we would work with the Seven Steps to see how he could further integrate everything covered in the session from the viewpoint of the Heart and pure consciousness. He readily agreed, and we met the following week.

In the next session, Jack and I concentrated on the Seven Steps. In the first Fours Steps, Jack contacted the spaciousness of Awareness, and was able to adapt the viewpoint of pure consciousness. This allowed him a neutral perspective to view everything we discussed in the previous session. In Step Five, he directly contacted his true nature as that Awareness, and it cleared the slate of his past history, placing him squarely into the heart of consciousness. He felt kindness arise within him, as he felt all his stories of judgement drop away. "Wow," he exclaimed, "am I going to be able to stay in this place all of the time?"

I told him that that was a possibility, but that something as precious as staying here at first sometimes does not come easily, but that the next Step was designed by Ramana Maharishi, to never leave this space.

If the reader recalls Step Six, it begins with a direct connection with pure awareness, and then watching the arising the arising of thoughts from this perspective. Jack followed my instruction to look at a thought as it rose from this pristine place of pure awareness. Then, he took each thought and in steps stripped it down until he was only left with the 'I' thought itself. This time, however, I was carefully watching my biofeedback readings, and when I saw his attention waver and knew that the mind had reappeared, I told him to come back to the 'I' thought and seek its source. I had Jack stay with this enquiry for almost five minutes, and then I told him to stop and relax.

"So, what did you experience?" I asked.

"It was like I was right there at the door, but then I would be somewhere else, thinking about something. Each time you brought me back to the enquiry, it would happen again."

"Jack, you ever watch a crime documentary or that movie *Cool Hand Luke,* where they have the tracking dogs and they follow the scent?"

"Yes, those dogs were amazing."

"Ramana Maharshi said that that is the way to follow the 'I' thought to its source, like a dog follows a scent. Once it gets a hold of it, it doesn't let go. You just experienced that it is not as easy as it sounds. Your attention wandered, didn't it?"

"Yes, it did."

"Jack, I can tell you value Radical Awakening. You came to me about the breakup of your marriage because it was disturbing what you had experienced. And you said your weakness is that your attention gets scattered and messes up other parts of your life.

Now I have tried to show you how important it is to keep attention concentrated in order to find the Source, to find out who you are. Ramana Maharshi, in giving this instruction, emphasized how it can only bring one to freedom if one had kept an unwavering focus on the true self while thoughts arise. Papaji said that to keep that focus required one thing: a true desire to be free. What he implied was that true desire would bring about a natural discipline to stay focused on the true self.

"I had never thought of it like that."

"When I am in India, I like to go to the temples in the evening. They are lit with ghee lamps and the local people come and offer flowers. They are dressed impeccably, especially the women and children. They walk around the shrine three times and then offer their flowers and receive the ash on their foreheads from the priest.

This is the life blood of Hinduism, the offering to God. It may seem formalistic, but there is a profound truth behind it. It is a symbol of the offering of our limitations to God, to the God that is to be realized as our very self. Perhaps you can see discipline as your offering to yourself, as your devotion to realizing God."

Jack was still. "Ramana, what you said is perfect, and I can feel it in my heart. Remember how I told you I didn't like the sound of the word discipline, but now it is different. When I see it as a gift, it becomes a part of me, deep inside, something precious even. As long as I have that point of view, I know I can do it. I just have to remember it if things get tough."

"Yes, remember it from the heart and it will work out."

"Thank you, Ramana. Thank you for everything."

"Jack, there is something more. We spent a lot of time on the breakup of your marriage. I am sure you understand what happened. You should do something with that understanding and make reparations to Adelle."

"You're right and I'll do that. I see that that is an important part of the process.

"Very good, now you've got it, Jack."

Crossroads Three: Self-Judgement and the Inability to Love Yourself Fully

It is inevitable that upon the path of awakening you will come face-to-face with your negative self-ego. The negative self-ego is the part of you that judges yourself harshly, and punishes you for the wrongs that you have done in your life.

But the negative self-ego is an imbalanced and an unreasonably harsh judge. My teacher of Alchemical Hypnotherapy, David Quigley, referred to this character as the 'hanging judge,' since ever sentence it declares heartlessly takes you to the gallows.

The negative self-ego preys on your regrets. We all have hurt people, or have hurt ourselves in ways that violated our personal moral codes, actions that we know in our hearts were wrong to do.

Our personal moral codes reach extends far beyond society's moral codes; they go to the very core of your personality. If there were actions that to you are unforgivable, even with the insight that you were not completely at fault. Although the mind readily comes in and justifies these actions, it can never completely cover up the fact that you know what you did was wrong.

The negative self-ego not only takes full advantage of your doubts, but it plays dirty. It not only judges your actions, but attacks your character; not only does it point out what you did was wrong, but also tells you how worthless as a person you are for doing it. On the surface, it may seem that the negative self-ego's admonitions have a good purpose: to make you feel so bad for what you did, that you would never do it again.

But in my work with trauma, I have found just the opposite occurs. Let me give you an example that may relate to something that happened in your own life.

Have you ever promised yourself that, in the height of your regret, that you will never, ever do that action again, only to find that later in life you are doing it again? Have you ever been so angry as child for being treated unfairly by your mother, make a decision that you will *never* be like your mother, only to find that as an adult, you are more like your mother than you care to admit? Ever wonder what that was about?

Since the negative self-ego blurs the lines between your actions and your character, your character become intricately associated with an unforgivable act. This results in obsessive self-doubt that paralyses and overwhelms the nervous system. That overwhelm creates another trauma, dissociation and unconsciousness, setting the stage for one to unconsciously act out again

Trauma presents itself in a cyclic nature. Although at times trauma overwhelms the nervous system, the body's defense mechanisms work to divert it whenever possible. t the time of those heart-felt promises to yourself, you are in so much pain and trauma that the mind will come up with anything to stop the pain.

These promises usually abates the pain, and the trauma of that incident gets repressed. Trauma is like a half-filled balloon that when you press the air out of the middle of the balloon, the two sides of the balloon burgeon out.

The trauma never goes anywhere when repressed, but only establishes itself in another place in the psyche. Although you may then feel better in the moment, the residue of the incident still hangs like a dark shadow in your general well-being, leaving your personal will in a compromised position.

You may find yourself not being able to really love yourself, since the negative self-ego continues to let you know of your worthlessness. When a new traumatic situation arises, the ego goes back to what it believes is the only option, and then next thing you know you are acting out again in harmful ways to yourself and to others. It is inevitable that a situation arises where the trauma resurfaces,

Upon inspection, you will find that the negative self-ego had a part in it, ready to judge and demean you yet another time.

From this perspective, the core of the judgements of the negative self-ego is a fundamental lie, and the truth is you are not the machinery of the personality and mind. Once the light of the true self is directly contacted, the purity of our true self emerges, and the lies of the negative self-ego are revealed.

Sadhana: **The 21-Days Yoga of Empowerment.**

(Note: this *sadhana* applies to each crossroads in this chapter.)

1) Begin by going through all 7 Steps in one sitting. This recording is titled "Your 70-Minutes Radical Awakening Session." When appropriate, use the crossroads in your life while doing so. That is, when you are asked to choose a thought or feeling, use the situation that is causing you distress.

2) After going through the recording, you will probably notice that one or two of the steps in particular helped you at your crossroads. For the following six days, listen to the recording of one of these steps. It can be the same step each day, or you can choose the other step. Approach each recording as a meditation practice. This practice will take you about ten to twenty minutes a day, depending on which Step you choose. It is best to set aside a specific time for meditation, preferably at the beginning or end of the day.

3) After completing your first seven days, repeat this program another two times, so that by the end of the *sadhana*, you have completed twenty-one days of meditation. However, you do not need to listen to your 70-Minutes Radical Awakening Session again. Each day you do only one Step.

About this *sadhana*:

This *sadhana* can seem like a lot to do. It really isn't, however. My personal sessions with people can go for a couple of hours, and often are so captivating so that the time passes easily. And remember, if you are at a major life-change crossroads, then your time will be well invested if you discover the heart and its guidance.

For some readers who already have a daily meditation practice, listening to a ten- to twenty-minute recording for twenty-one days will seem like child's play. Regardless, this twenty-one days *sadhana* will reap rewards for anyone.

Approach the initial seventy-minutes recording as if you were scheduling a private session with me. Recordings are always made of my Radical Awakening sessions, and many people tell me that they receive as much or even more benefit from listening to the recording as from their original session. Similarly, this opportunity to go through your Radical Awakening again, in one complete session, will surprise you with how much you learn from it.

Using the charged thoughts and feelings associated with your crossroads during the seventy-minutes recording can be a powerful release. The ensuing daily ten- to twenty-minute meditations (depending on which Step you choose) reinforce and deepen what opened for you in the seventy-minutes session.

By the end of this *sadhana* you should know the Steps well enough that you will no longer need the audio recordings and will be able to apply them as you go through your daily life. You may also discover that when persistent negative thoughts or feelings are released, the energy bound up in them is also released and transforms into more energy and power in your life. In time, you will find it natural to let stressful thoughts and feelings dissipate into the magic of space.

Beyond the Crossroads: Finding a Home in the Cave of the Heart

The reality is that life is filled with crossroads. Even after a Radical Awakening, our reflex may be to contract, to put a shell around the heart, to be "right" and make others "wrong." Fortunately, the Self always wants to know itself, and love always wants to express itself.

Regardless of our latent tendencies, after an Awakening, there is a new and palpable attraction to rest in the Heart of Consciousness. Here, there exists the possibility to stabilize and deepen into a total state of freedom.

There comes the point when we find that peace does not stem from this world. We realize there is nowhere else to go, but into the existence of Pure Love. Our attention continually needs to return to love, because there's nowhere else to go. The return to love takes us to the Cave of the Heart, where we seek refuge from the maelstrom of life's experiences, a place of sanctuary from within.

Lay not up for yourselves treasures upon the earth, where moth and rust do corrupt, and where thieves break through and steal. But lay up for yourselves treasures in heaven, where neither moth nor rust doth corrupt, and where thieves do not break through nor steal. For where thy treasure is, there will thy heart be also.

– St. Francis of Assisi

CHAPTER 5
Opening to the Heart of Consciousness

*P*revious chapters have provided guidance about common circumstances that can arise immediately following your Radical Wakening session. That advice is meant both to reassure you and to help you over the speed bumps that can emerge upon awakening. The situations we examine in greater depth throughout this section are all opportunities to guide us at certain inevitable junctions of Awakening. In a sense, each crossroad is a further nexus where Awakening can deepen. The situations that follow are challenging. One does not easily make decisions about which direction to take right away. Neither path is "good" or "bad." They are only different. Life will continue presenting moments like these as many times as it likes, no matter which way we choose. And we are completely free to choose our road. To follow the mind produces one set of consequences, and to follow the heart produces another.

Since following the mind is already habitual, this chapter considers what can happen by choosing the path of the heart. As Ramana Marhashi has said, "*The 'Heart' is the seat of Consciousness itself.*" Again, the ideas discussed here are not meant to show that one way is "right," while another is "wrong." The chapter simply provides you with new options to explore after your Radical Awakening. Our awareness of Awakening is a recursive process; however, by choosing the Heart more and more frequently, we can cultivate our connection to the purity of the True Self with greater consciousness and understanding.

·eeling Everything Fully and Completely

.t crossroad of Awakening is one at which we decide between accepting everything that life presents, "good" or "bad," or only accepting what we would prefer to. The choice may seem obvious, but it's often much more complicated than we realize. It's easy to fool ourselves into believing that we've chosen the path of the heart, when in reality, the mind has slipped on a new outfit and called itself "spiritual."

We are familiar with the stereotype of a "truly spiritual person," residing on a mountaintop, meditating in a cave. Indeed, a sage like Ramana Maharshi did just that. We must recall, however, that a very particular set of spiritual, geographical and cultural circumstances led his life to manifest that way. The rest of us have different sets of conditions that lead our Awakenings to manifest in infinite forms. Most importantly, however, _if we think that we will live free of disruptive feelings and responsibilities upon the mountaintop, we are wrong_. Ramana Maharshi never escaped emotional states or duties. Similarly, life does not spare us, whether we are on the mountain, or not. In the end, we all face the inevitability of managing life on its terms: its ups and downs, its miracles and disappointments, its victories and defeats. Simply put, there is no escaping the fullness of life, experiencing it all—even the parts we wish to reject.

The secret to working through the hard parts lies in the infinite space of Pure Consciousness. When we are upset, for example, we tend to feel the intensity of emotion, not only in the mind but within the body as well. Some people have "nervous stomachs," while others may be prone to headaches or backaches. Regardless of where you store your tension, when you realize the infinite space of Consciousness, if only briefly, it allows for the intensity of feelings to dissipate into that boundless space. Gradually, those feelings are no longer confined to the body, as we usually experience them. The energy generated from the emotions can be released, opening a space for us to feel everything completely. In other words, sadness can be an invitation to investigate our ability to accept everything at the moment, just as it is.

In 2002, I experienced something that demonstrated the profound link between allowing an unwanted feeling and an opportunity to experience enlightenment. Of all places, it occurred while I was lying in a hospital bed in Bangkok.

On my yearly pilgrimages to India, I often stopover in Southern Thailand to fulfill my love of rock climbing. While climbing an easy rock face, one which I would sometimes even climb without a rope, I took a fall that broke my tibia in several places. I was rushed to a hospital in Bangkok and immediately taken into surgery. A metal plate was put in my lower leg to secure the broken pieces of my shinbone together.

After the operation, the doctors informed me that I would be in recovery for four or five days until the swelling went down in my leg. Part of this recovery would involve being given pain medication several times, both day and night. I was asked to indicate the level of my pain through a series of illustrations on the wall that went from a person smiling to someone crying.

Throughout my recovery time, I noticed feeling a diffuse sensation that spread out from my broken leg, into the larger space of the room. Rather than feeling an intense and concentrated pain in the immediate area of the injury, everything expanded instead of contracting. During my stay in the hospital, I always pointed to the person smiling and therefore was never given any pain medication. My lack of pain, as well as the fact that my swelling came down in half the anticipated time, baffled both the doctors and nurses.

Like the first step in a Radical Awakening process, when awareness is invited to magnify, all constricted feelings are dispersed into a larger space. When my consciousness naturally expanded out, rather than folding in on the pain, I felt drawn to explore the *subtleties* of what I was feeling. By doing so, the intensity of my pain seemed to dilute itself throughout my focus.

To provide a more visual analogy, the area of the injury was a giant red spot on a piece of blotting paper. If a few tablespoons of water were to be spilled directly over that red spot, the ink would spread out. It would dilute into a fading pink splotch, its most outer edges perhaps a darker hue of red-pink. In this comparison, the ink spreading out over the paper represents the intensity of the pain attenuating and moving out over a larger space.

In my case, my attention was drawn to the sensations at the *outer edges* of the pain in my leg, just as the pinkish-red water mark inched away from its originally bright center. From this periphery, I experienced the subtleties of sensations, which I would otherwise have felt as "pain." There was no conscious intention to expand into these sensations; I was irresistibly *drawn* to them.

When the process ended, I had felt all the sensations within the space of my leg, the bed, the room, the hospital, and beyond. All that remained was the infinite space of Pure Consciousness. The swelling stopped in a fraction of the time anticipated, and I was discharged from the hospital.

It later occurred to me that when you take away the *story* around the sensations you are feeling, there is no real difference between *emotional pain* and *physical pain*. Without the *story* connecting them, both are reduced to sensations running through the body (there was an exercise demonstrating this concept in *Section I,* Chapter 4*).* The result was a naturally occurring absence of resistance, accompanied by an invitation to experience *any* feelings that arose.

I tell this story, not to dismiss the difficulty of living with other types of pain that may be chronic and acute, whatever their source. Nor is it to make light of circumstances so shattering that they leave us emotionally and physically immobilized. All such situations can certainly drive us to dark and challenging places. Medical intervention, or appropriate mental health intercession, are fitting primary responses to certain circumstances. Rather, I share my story only to illustrate what is possible, and to give hope to those who are at any stage of emotional or physical pain. I hope that my example shows that there are measures that can provide additional relief in otherwise intractable situations.

Another version of a crossroad between mind and heart can occur when a person who has had a Radical Awakening bumps up against either a personal sense of injustice or social and global injustices as a whole. I often see people struggling to accept something that they feel is unacceptable or wrong. These include war, tyranny, torture of the innocent, cruelty to animals, or contributing to environmental destruction, for example. When it comes to highly volatile topics such as these, however, people often feel torn. On the one hand, they feel that they must "accept" these matters, to be truly "spiritual"; on the contrary, they find it morally reprehensible to sit in the face of injustice and do nothing. Now, it feels like the Universe has handed them an impossible decision to make at such a crossroad.

A usual tactic when a spiritual seeker, even one who has had a Radical Awakening, faces such conflicts is to *suppress* his feelings of disdain, rejection or judgments. This suppression is made possible by conjuring up an image of himself as a person of "higher consciousness," which gives rise to what is called in spirituality, an "enlightened ego." The "enlightened ego" pontificates about spiritual truths, while its heart is cloaked in judgment, righteousness, and superiority. The "enlightened ego," is not fooling anyone but himself.

Fortunately, we can sidestep this whole egoic cycle at the crossroad by following the direction of Pure Consciousness. When chosen often enough, we learn that this acceptance of the "now" is no longer something that a person *does*, but is something that arises organically. The elimination of desires and resistances is something that cannot be done at an intellectual level, or with any sense of effort. *It all happens outside of the sphere of the one who is resisting.* The personality that formerly felt the need to suppress doesn't even *choose* to stop "suppressing." It just merges into the Heart of Awareness.

A person who is in an enlightened state is often described as one who embraces everything, and resists nothing — they are always fully present. In other words, what if each time a resistance were present, it could be *drawn* and absorbed into the infinite space of Awareness? The presence of that resistance would dismantle itself and naturally fall away. would be completely experienced; nothing would be left out.

This realization shifted my view of who and what an enlightened person was. Before this investigation, I considered a truly enlightened person as one who was above it all, and emotionally collected. He would experience nothing but bliss and peace in every moment.

I then realized that I had everything upside down. I saw that a fully enlightened person embraces the openness with an infinite heart, which therefore *allows* him to feel everything deeply, without attachment. This non-attachment then permits him, in an appropriate manner, to *express* the *entire* range of human emotions. In other words, there is no "Manual for Enlightened People," let alone a chapter in it that restricts you to experiencing only "spiritual" feelings. No longer misidentified with the suffering of a separate sense of self, there remains a deep connectedness to the enlightened one's ability to feel the full range of human emotion, indeed the wholeness of humanity.

What changes is the motivation of acting on any particular issue. Judgements are replaced my an awareness of connectedness, and a person can then be drawn to take the appropriate steps from Heart rather than from mental concepts.

Living an Authentic Life

Living an authentic life requires us to be completely honest with ourselves. When we encounter situations that don't fit in with how we perceive ourselves, or how we want others to see us, we actively begin editing our actions and thoughts. This editing process distorts our ability to experience things authentically and increases our ability to repress what we don't to experience.

Bottled-up emotions don't just disappear, though. Instead, they express themselves in other ways. For instance, if we repress our anger towards someone, it can show up later as passive aggression, or in covertly hostile acts. When we suppress loss, it can throw a blanket over *all* of our emotions, leaving us with a feeling of dullness. Symptomatic patterns can show up as avoidance, overeating, being overly preoccupied with work, or zoning out in front of the television. The most common way to avoid feeling sensations is to distract ourselves with judgment, irritation, and impatience.

This repression does not allow us to experience the full range of human emotions, leaving only an audited, narrow bandwidth with which to interface with the world and ourselves. This repression of emotions is often followed by unconscious and hurtful actions—whether towards others, or ourselves. Ultimately, this repression separates us from the *essence* of all forms of life in the universe. Our hearts become blocked.

All emotions, including ones that are repressed or blocked, are stored in a place I call the *Heart of Emotions*. In the meditations I lead, it is not unusual for people to feel their emotions, perhaps even for the first time. Sometimes people become uncomfortable in these meditations. When touching the *Heart of Emotions*, they begin to feel things they had previously repressed, such as regret, remorse, guilt, fear, and anger.

The source of these blocked feelings typically stems from early childhood traumatic incidents, when a developing, fragile ego became overwhelmed with emotions. The mind's defense system kept the individual safe by steering them away from anything that would remind them of the traumatic experience.

Rather than re-experiencing any aspect of the incident, the mind diverts attention by engaging in intellectual problem-solving. It actively tries to control and manage any part of a situation that might elicit an unwanted emotional feeling or response.

We then construct a complicated story about *those other people* and how they are wrong, which we support by using a bank of "facts" and slanted observations. Heavy judgments cloaked in "spiritual discrimination" conclude that *those other people* are fundamentally unethical, self-centered, lazy and hypocrites. In truth, *those other people* are simply being themselves. It just so happens they are triggering emotions that the one suppressing his feelings does not want to feel. Of course, none of this is seen by the one who is suppressing the feelings. He is so wrapped up in his story that all he can experience is his irritation and lack of control.

A person could have an image in his head that he is an easy-going, live-and-let-live kind of person, while his actions could be demanding and opinionated, and his viewpoints rigid. If input from others does not fit into his self-created image, then that feedback from others is summarily rejected.

To be in tune with Source, you must choose to become one with life, rather than at war with life. The energy it previously took to suppress emotions can then be released into a natural response to whatever is unfolding in the moment. We never have to "work on" accepting troublesome situations. Rather, those situations don't even show up on the radar as "troublesome." Consciousness rejects nothing, nor does it label things as "good" or "bad." If you feel inspired to respond to an authentic call to action, do so. If you want to join a group that works to save an endangered species or volunteer at a woman's shelter, do so. There are countless valuable endeavors to engage in that respond to the many inequities of our world. At the same time, however, there is equal merit in finding more equanimity and peace in situations that were previously difficult. You can move more authentically to help solve these injustices when you move from a golden heart, in tandem with a clear mind. The bird needs both wings to fly.

Surrendering to the Vulnerability of Loving

A third crossroad we all come to is the crossroad of the broken heart. The cautious mind tends to measure out love in small parcels, to ensure that the heart never gets broken. To this guarded mind, surrendering to the vulnerability of love is a sure path to emotional disaster. If the watchful mind were successful with this strategy, however, nobody would ever have a broken heart.

Of course, heartbreaks come in many forms; they can be triggered by romantic loss, the death of a loved one, a tragedy that affects ourselves, or our community. A broken heart can happen at any age, and over any situation that matters deeply to us. As much as we'd like to control issues of the heart, our brokenness usually emerges out of a situation that is out of our control, and beyond all of our attempts to change things. When it becomes clear that surrender is not only the *wisest* option but our *only* option, then the heart is paradoxically ripe for a breakthrough.

When our hearts break, it can be a powerful catalyst for self-reflection and a search for deeper truths. Without the raw vulnerability that arises from such pain, it is nearly impossible to embrace any truth that is more important than our "story." Both fortunately, and unfortunately, these moments can be the most authentically transformative in our lives. As a result, they offer opportunities with no equal in the range of human emotion.

If we re-frame the heartbreak itself, there is a chance to see it through a different lens than the traditional ones ingrained into our respective societies and cultures. In some civilizations, for example, a broken heart is not a condition to avoid, but rather a condition for growth. Put differently, the cultural frame around the concept of *heartbreak* can differ from society to society. In 1991, for example, I conducted a joint yoga/*Satsang* Retreat in Tulum, a walled city on the Yucatan coast. Part of the afternoons were spent exploring the Mayan ruins in the area. One day, we happened upon a Mayan elder who offered to be our guide. As we explored the area, his knowledge of ancient Mayan culture grew more apparent, as did his personal wisdom.

Before we parted that day, I pulled him aside and spoke to him privately about his mention of the *Popul-Vuh*, a sacred religious text of the early Mayans, sometimes referred to as the "Mayan Bible." I wanted to know so much more about this book than time allowed, so I asked him this: "If you could summarize the primary message of the Mayan Bible, what would it be?" He thought for a moment, and replied, "That is a big question! I would like to go and meditate on it for a while. Let me get back to you tomorrow, and I will let you know what comes to me."

The next day, he shared with me what his meditation revealed as the primary message of this Holy Scripture: "*Keep your heart broken.*"

In hearing his answer, I knew that I had just received an enlightened transmission. Twenty five years later, I continue to discover the wisdom of those four simple words.

A heartbreak requires us to feel in ways that we usually don't allow ourselves to experience. In truth, it propels us to *make peace* with a heart that is breaking or broken. It teaches us to surrender everything to it. This submission generates a state of genuine trust in something larger than ourselves. It is in this state of graceful trust that the gift of a broken heart is at last realized.

Unity between vulnerability and strength dance in this realization. The Heart of Consciousness *is* that unity. It allows us to be exposed enough to give and to receive love completely. This integration frees us from the power of the ego and the limitations of personality. We discover ourselves as unbounded freedom, and we live in a state of complete surrender.

This surrender, in turn, engenders a different kind of vulnerability. It is no longer the kind that emanates from the grief of injury, but a quiet and *natural* acceptance of what life is giving us. We accept everything thoroughly and comprehensively. In feeling so deeply, we contact the intensifying love that splinters through the feeble protective layer the foolish mind tried to create in the first place. It is through this breaking that Divine light infuses the soul, and illuminates it with the very thing we feared: love itself.

Awakening to the True You as Purity Itself

This crossroad is one at which we choose either to move through a familiar motion habitually or to do so consciously, from the Heart. Although relatively straightforward by comparison to the other junctures mentioned above, it's important because of its direct ability to remind us of the Truth of Who we Are. In India, the recognition of the purity of the True Self is expressed through the Sanskrit word, *Namasté*. The most common definition of *Namasté* in the West is "the God within me bows to the God within you." The Sanskrit word, *Nama* (the first part of the word, *Namasté*) means to "bow," or "surrender to." But what is the deeper meaning of this "God within us"?

Ancient Sanskrit scripture speaks of a sacred flame, called "*Agni*," that burns so hot that anything that comes to it is transformed into a pure substance. Ramana Maharshi often said,

"The true Self lives in the heart of all living beings. The real self embodies the purity of the sacred flame, and is therefore considered to be an aspect of our true Selves."

In performing the gesture that accompanies this greeting, the shape of the *Namasté* hand position, as well as *where* we place it, are both necessary. The hand position is shaped similarly to that of a candle flame.

This sacred flame resides in the Heart. By squarely placing the hands over the *heart chakra*, we directly contact the purity of the True Self, abiding in the heart.

Sometimes this *Namasté* hand gesture is put over the *third eye* (the spot between the eyebrows). This placement signifies that this flame is purifying our inner seeing.

Sometimes the hand gesture of *Namasté* is positioned on the lips. Bringing the sacred flame to our lips purifies our tongue and speech. Whether placed over the *third eye* or the lips, it always begins and ends in the position over the heart, where the True Self abide

In this way, when we bow in the gesture of *namasté*, we honor the sacred purity of *"Agni."* It is also a surrender to the truth of Who We Really Are. Take a moment right now to put your hands in the *namasté* position over your heart and go within. Here, you can feel the sacredness and purity of your own True Heart.

The Sacred Flame and the Holy Mountain *Arunachala Shiva*

This same sacred flame is also known as the *Aarti* flame and has been used in ancient India as far back as 50,000 years, or more. In India today, this *Aarti* flame is still used in sacred ceremonies to bring forth this revered light and spiritual purification.

In every Hindu temple in India, there is a representation of this sacred fire. The light from this fire embodies Absolute Consciousness and in the form representing an infinite column of purifying light is known as a *Shiva Lingam*. The term *Shiva* appears in the ancient writings of the *Vedas* and is described as the primary principle of Absolute Consciousness. In the ancient teachings of the Indian *Puranas* (the stories of the Indian Gods), this *Shiva Lingam* is said to exist in the physical world, in the form of a mountain in Southern India called *Arunachala Shiva* (sometimes just called, *Arunachala*). It is said that this sacred mountain, the physical and energetic embodiment of *Lord Shiva*, manifests itself as a giant pillar of purity, fire, and light (a natural *Shiva Lingam*).

The *Arunachala Puranas* further state that "even to think of *Arunachala* purifies the mind, or to hear about *Arunachala* purifies the ears, and to behold *Arunachala* purifies the eyes." These verses demonstrate the cultural power of this purifying force.

Ramana Maharshi, in his most celebrated piece of literature, "The Marital Garland of Verses," states, "*Oh, Arunachala, thou dost root out the ego in all who meditate on thee in the heart.*" He further states that "*Arunachala* is the source of a <u>silent transmission</u>, which quiets the mind and opens the heart."

The energy of *Arunachala* peaks during a ten-day celebration called *Karthigai Deepam*. It takes place when the full moon is in conjunction with the star system *Karthigai,* also known as the Pleiades. In Sanskrit, *Deepam* is another word for *Agni*. The earliest references to this festival date back to 300 BCE; it was considered to be one of the most important holy ceremonies by the Ancient peoples of South India.

In preparation for this festival, an enormous sacred cauldron is placed on the highest of *Arunachala's* five peaks and filled with ghee. A torch is lit from a flame that has been burning for hundreds of years inside the main *Shiva* temple. This flame is then relayed by hand up the 1,000-meter mountain face to the awaiting cauldron, positioned on its summit. At precisely six o'clock, as the sun sets and the full moon rises, the sacred cauldron is lit, as hundreds of thousands of eyes watch in pious silence. This sacred fire remains lit for the duration of the 10-day celebration; its massive flame can be seen as far as 23 kilometers away. Hundreds of thousands of ghee lamps are also lit all around the mountain.

During the 24-hour period in which the *Karthigai Deepam* Moon waxes into fullness, over a million people circle the perimeter of *Arunachala* to receive the grace of its silent transmission. Ramana Maharshi stated that circling Arunachala *"removes karma, fulfills true desires, gives freedom from future births and grants liberation."*

To find out about our annual pilgrimage to Arunachala click below

http://www.radicalawakening.org/India/ArunachalaMenu.html

CHAPTER 6
Building Your Spiritual "Tool Belt"

As a young boy, I was a great fan of the comic book action hero, Batman. The caped crusader's formula for success seemed intimately connected to his remarkable "utility belt." Through the eyes of a child, it appeared to be the mystical Swiss Army knife of belts. When Batman wanted to swing from building to building, he grabbed his bat rope with its hook, and he was off. When he needed explosives, he reached into that belt and "Pow!" "Bam!""Boom!" – explosions happened at precisely the right moment.

It was evident that he knew his tools, and he knew exactly where they were on his belt. He knew them so well, in fact, that it was an automatic response for him to reach for the right device, at the right moment. He never paused to consider, "Hmmm. Now, I need my bat listening device. Now, I need my bat boomerang." Whatever he needed, he went for it instinctively.

In this chapter, we present strategic tools for you to build your own 'spiritual toolbelt'. These tools are designed to help you to apply your awakening experience to the challenges of your everyday life. And like Batman, through repetition, your access to these tools can be immediate and automatic.

The thing that distinguishes Batman from other superheroes is that he doesn't possess any inherent superpowers. Instead, he uses his thorough mastery of his tools to move through each new challenge.

Although there are some like Ramana Maharshi, who experience an Awakening that instantly leads to a permanent state of Enlightenment, most of us are more like Batman: just a regular person who skillfully uses a variety of "tools" to cope with the scoundrels of Gotham City. Although there's no single way to eliminate these rogue difficulties as they appear in our lives, there are instruments we can use to help us along the way. Knowing that every tool will not necessarily work for every person or in every situation, this chapter offers a range of practices to consider.

The following are five tools for your 'bat utility belt. Although you have experienced a Radical Awakening, it is inevitable that circumstance will arise which trigger your conditioned, habitual ego-response. That is when you will find these tools useful.

With patience and vigilance, a new habit of mind will form. More and more, we will notice that the new response will become natural. No longer will the tools in this chapter be just an intellectual tactic to deal better with our frustrations and challenges. They will become an automatic and useful response.

Ideally, the tools will evolve so that they will no longer be separate from us, but rather a part of us. Once we reach a stable level of Pure Consciousness, where the Divine flows through us without the agitation of mind or ego, the need for any tools drops away.

Tool #1: Foreground / Background Exercise

The quality of our experience is determined by how and where we place our attention. When we place it mainly on Pure Consciousness, that Consciousness moves to the foreground of experience. When our attention shifts to the world of objects, Pure Consciousness moves further into the background of our awareness. When awareness of consciousness moves far into the background, we often mistake it for no longer being present. This creates the *illusion* of Awareness "coming and going."

It bears repeating that this is not the movement of Awareness itself, but rather the movement of our *experience* of it.

In Illustration 4-1 (below), Pure Consciousness (depicted by a heart, flower, and rainbow) is in both the foreground and the background of experience. Jane is happy and feels at peace.

Illustration 4-1: Jane enjoys the direct perception of Pure Consciousness

However, when Jane is distracted by something, she no longer experiences the happiness and peace. Her attention pivots entirely to what is happening in the moment (see illustration 4-2, below). In this case, she is having an argument with another person.

Illustration 4-2: Then a challenge arises

As this moment unfolds, Jane's attention is primarily focused on the argument in the foreground of her experience. When that focus occupies most of her awareness, Pure Consciousness is something far in the background of awareness (see illustration 4-3, below).

Illustration 4-3: Pure Consciousness far in the background of consciousness (indicated by the heart, rainbow and flower being grayed out)

These are the situations in which the refinement of our awareness is needed to effect change. Jane notices what she previously missed: Awareness is still present, only far, far in the background. By stopping for a moment and scanning for the **ever-present** Pure Awareness, she discovers Its presence. Although this Presence is in the background of experience as a small part of her awareness, she can rest in this Consciousness.

In Illustration 4-4 (below), we see that the argument remains dominant in the foreground, while a part of her is simultaneously at peace, resting in the small area of Pure Awareness. That small area of Pure Awareness is the calm eye in the middle of the storm.

Illustration 4-4: Finding peace in the tiny space inside the background of awareness.

The purpose of this tool is to develop the skill to recognize the Presence of Awareness even when it is small and far in the background. This recognition softens the quality of your day-to-day experience.

Instructions for the Foreground / Background Tool:

For one-half second, stop everything. Scan for the **ever-present** Pure Awareness. Notice the presence of Awareness, even if it is far, far in the background of your experience. When It is contacted, notice the subtle shift in perception.

At this juncture, the scales tip, and Pure Consciousness begins expanding into the foreground of our attention. We find ourselves responding to the events in our daily lives from a broader perspective.

Over time, we become more and more drawn into this expanded state of Awareness. As we progress in our spiritual development, we gradually move our attention to the larger picture of expanded space.

This shift takes practice. If things are going just the way we want them to, we will have less motivation to practice this tool. It is within our biggest storms that a true spiritual aspirant is driven deeper into the center of the storm. It is during these times of turmoil that this tool becomes essential.

We can be fully engaged in life while resting in Consciousness. Whatever happens in the circumstances around us, we can be at rest in the eye of the storm.

Tool #2: The Oscilloscope Exercise Tool

This exercise uses the analogy of an oscilloscope, an instrument through which a fluctuating electrical current can temporarily be seen as a visible waveform on a screen. The sign waves on the oscilloscope move up into a "positive" space, and down into a "negative" space. For our purposes, we will think of these waves as representing positive and negative experiences in our lives that happen moment by moment.

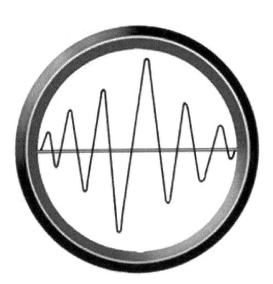

Illustration 4-5: The Oscilloscope

If we look at the center of the screen showing this movement, we see a permanently etched-in line that runs through the sine waves from left to right. It separates the upper positive portions of the waves from the lower negative portions. That line represents the "zero point," where the sine wave comes up from the negative space, hitting zero before it goes into the positive space.

The static line only moves in one direction, showing the passage of time, always at zero and always already present. Here, there is no movement up and down. For us, this etched-in line represents *the space that does not move, yet the space in which all things move*. This "zero point" is a point of stillness and centeredness. It's where the silent witness, the "seer," resides.

This "seer" is the Self that does not participate in the experiences appearing on the screen, but rather witnesses those experiences. Throughout every moment of our lives, from our highest mood to our lowest mood, this stationary line remains constant throughout each cycle. There is no place on the timeline where this "zero point" does not exist.

In our model, this ever-present line represents Pure Consciousness. Even though experiences change, we start realizing that the presence of Pure Consciousness, which is the True Perceiver, is always there and is always perceiving.

Because the motionless line is not in the realm of experience, from that "zero point," we may step back and observe the waves of our experiences– good, bad, or indifferent. This stepping back enables us to be in our lives, but to watch the waves of our undertakings and exchanges in a whole new way.

We eliminate the rigid patterns of behavior we felt locked into at an earlier stage. Instead, we become more willing to experience acceptance and joy about the way things are, whatever that may be. Additionally, when needed, the action comes from a place of greater clarity and creativity.

Instructions for the Oscilloscope Tool:

*Close your eyes and find the quiet place within, below the level of thoughts. Let your attention rest in that calm center. Anchor that tranquility in the Heart.

*Open your eyes but stay within, keeping part of your attention on the peacefulness of the Heart.

*Go throughout your life with greater and greater attention to the quiet, calm, heartfelt space.

Tool #3: The Sound Track Exercise

In this exercise, we discover the connections between thoughts and emotions. Our experience tells us that they're inseparable. However, we will find that they're not **innately** connected. This fact gives us the ability to separate our thoughts and emotions, keeping the negative ones from escalating.

It is important at this juncture to make the distinction between three commonly interchangeable terms: **sensations, feelings, and emotions**. When we encounter a situation that evokes anger, we first experience a series of sensations: a constriction in the solar-plexus, a tightening of the shoulders, and an acceleration of the breath.

These are **sensations** or **feelings** experienced by the body. This combination of feelings/sensations creates a specific profile that the mind then interprets as the **emotion** of "anger."

Let's examine this Cycle of Emotional Escalation in slow motion. The body's alert system is triggered, and the mind does what it does best: it tries to figure out what's wrong, and how to fix it. A story evolves quickly about what "should" or "should not" be, and why.

The mind scans whose fault it is, and once it identifies a guilty party, it further increases the feelings/sensations in the body. Within milliseconds, the mind interprets the constellation of sensations to be anger. This *further* escalates the feelings and sensations within the body. The nervous system becomes overwhelmed. Suddenly, everything is out of control.

It's important to note that The Cycle of Emotional Escalation can begin from the opposite direction as well; that is, instead of being triggered by a sensation in the body, the trigger can occur due to an *outside* event.

In this case, someone may just slip in front of you with 25 items in the 10-item quick-check line; a teenager won't put his dirty clothes in the hamper; or, a spouse refuses to put the cap back on the toothpaste. The cycle is still the same. No matter how it starts--either through an internal sensation or an outside event--the feedback loop is just as slippery.

To provide an example of how this cycle works, let's first consider the scenario of a young woman who absentmindedly walks into the edge of her coffee table, producing a sensation of sharp pain at the top of her left kneecap. Her mind immediately follows the unwelcome sting with a series of thoughts; in fact, those ideas come so quickly that they're virtually simultaneous with the acute sensation registering in her brain. "Oh, stupid, stupid! Why did I do that? It had to be my left knee, my bad knee, always my bad knee! Nice. How am I supposed to go for a run this afternoon with this? I'm never going to lose this weight and find a husband! It's hopeless. Something is always working against me. I can't do anything right..."

With this story in mind, let's consider the way a traditional film reel works. All the images run down the center of the filmstrip, while the soundtrack--voices, music, sound effects, and volume control--is located beside the visual material. If we apply this concept to the scenario above, when we separate the images on the filmstrip from all the chatter, noise, and thoughts, the "silent movie" that would play on the screen would show nothing more than a "young woman banging her knee on a coffee table." That's it. That's all we would see.

However, if we reinsert her mental soundtrack alongside that innocuous event, it quickly escalates in her mind to a *story* about her recklessness that has dashed her hopes of ever losing weight, finding a husband and living a fulfilled life. Suddenly, "young woman bangs knee on coffee table" becomes a tale of self-induced tragedy and lifelong loneliness.

The *Sound Track Exercise* enables us to separate the mind's commentary from direct sensation, eliminating the phase of mental interpretation. This elimination allows us to discover that feelings literally can't take shape, let alone escalate when the *story* is taken away.

In Illustration 4-6 we see "the voice speaking inside the head" is playing movie soundtracks of anger, fear, loss, or unfulfilled desires.

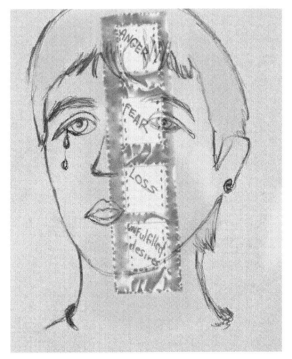

Illustration 4-6: Soundtrack Inside the Head

Illustration 4-7 demonstrates The Cycle of Escalating Emotions. As mentioned above, the cycle can start in the gut or the head. Here, the "movie soundtrack" plays in the head, setting off the body's alert system that something is wrong. The nervous system becomes flooded with feelings and sensations, which then commands the mind to categorize, label and assess the situation, to figure out how to stop it.

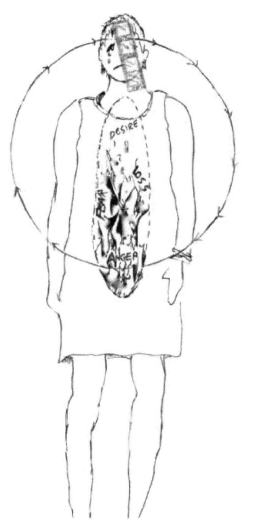

Illustration 4-7: The Cycle of Escalating Emotions

The cycle eventually escalates to the point where the nervous system goes into overwhelm (Illustration 4-8).

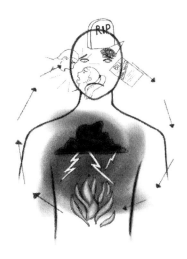

Illustration 4-8: Emotional Overwhelm

However, as seen in Illustration 4-9, when the filmstrip is removed from the woman's head and placed in space to her right, the cycle of suffering ends. Removing the mind's soundtrack bypasses the cycle of escalation, keeping the nervous system from going into overwhelm. It's now possible to "be with" your feelings. Or, as we commonly refer to it in this work, it allows you to "feel everything deeply."

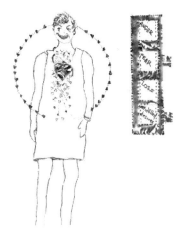

Illustration 4-9: The Soundtrack outside of the body

Instructions for the Soundtrack Tool:

*Stop for a moment and become alert to Awareness perceiving the soundtrack of your movie.

*Remove the soundtrack from your head and place it beside you (to the left or the right, whichever side feels more comfortable to you). There should be a release of tension once the soundtrack is completely "outside" the body.

*Explore any sensations in the body. Pay particular attention to where the sensations are located in the body. Explore how you experience pure sensation or feeling, devoid of stories or labels.

*Allow yourself the time to experience your feelings fully. Sink deep into what is present. Keep your attention on that presence as you go throughout your day until you're aware of it, through and through.

Why the Soundtrack Exercise Works

According to Harvard-trained and published neuroanatomist, Dr. Jill Bolte Taylor, recent neurological research has shown that emotions, without a story, can only last for approximately 90 seconds– a rather startling discovery. She explains that human neurocircuitry is such that when we first think a "thought," it elicits an "emotion."

The corresponding part of the brain, such as the amygdale's role in the emotion of anger, responds with particular neuro-stimulating chemicals. The crux of Taylor's argument is that the same neurochemicals that rapidly flood the bloodstream after an emotional trigger, also *flush themselves out* of the body just as quickly. In this way, Dr. Taylor's research shows that the time it takes to think a thought to the time when the bloodstream can be *entirely clean* of all that chemistry is less than 90 seconds.

The observation above means that if we carry any emotion, such as anger, for more than a minute and a half, it can *only* be because we're replaying the *story* of the event in the mind, which simultaneously triggers and repeats the chemical response. If we keep repeating it long enough, we not only remain in a negative emotional space, but the body itself experiences the sensations of that anger, again and again. When thoughts and sensations are no longer fueling one another, the emotional charge falls out of the feedback loop, and the story loses its power and significance. Moreover, Dr. Taylor's research also reminds us that we are physiologically capable of developing the mindfulness to watch and interrupt this cycle at any time.

The Sound-Track Exercise follows the rules of all emergency medical care: The sooner the intervention occurs, the better the results. This exercise teaches us to detect the early signs of impending overwhelm. By identifying an emergency quickly, we can move, like Batman, and instinctively grab this tool early in the cycle of overwhelm. If we can use this tool skillfully, we can learn to refine our "early detection warning system," and will eventually find it useful every time.

Tool #4: The Trapdoor to the Heart

Without realizing it, we all tend to concentrate our vital energy in our cranium, the logical spot from which we assume thoughts grow. What would happen, however, if we were to move all that energy and attention from the head, and put it onto the area of the Heart chakra instead? This tool is a way to drop into the Heart, swiftly and efficiently. Here, we explore how by putting our attention on the True Heart, rather than on thoughts, the quality of our experiences is dramatically altered.

After acknowledging the energy of thoughts in the head, as discussed above, we move to the crucial juncture of the neck. The symbolism of the neck holds a vital place in history since more than one great person has unwillingly lost his head via that stalk. Here, however, we will happily "lose our heads," if only metaphorically.

Because thoughts invariably seem to take up all the space in the head, one pull of a "trap door" in the neck allows all those ideas to flow down into the Infinite Heart of the True Self. Here, thoughts are transformed immediately into silence, love, and joy.

Instructions for the Trap Door to the Heart Tool:

*Imagine that there is a trap door at the top of your neck, and when the trap door gets pulled, all of the thoughts that are filling your head, start to fall toward the heart (see Illustration 4-10, below).

Illustration 4:10 Pulling the trapdoor to the Heart

Become aware of the infinite nature of Love and the Heart. Let all of your thoughts fall into that vastness (see Illustration 4-11, below).

Illustration 4-11: Thoughts falling into the Infiniteness of Heart

Tool #5: Prayer

Prayer is a deeply personal matter. Not everyone believes in prayer, and even those who do may not engage in the practice regularly, or even occasionally. It is also defined in almost as many ways as there are religions and spiritual beliefs. Some consider prayer as a last-ditch effort. Some consider it a practice that requires bargaining for a request– by giving up a particular habit or promising to engage in another– in return for the wish granted. Others believe it must happen in a particular form, in a particular place, or at a given time, to be valid. Here, we honor everyone's beliefs and thoughts on this delicate matter. The exercise simply invites one to consider the practice from a radically different perspective, regardless of the reader's starting point. In no way does the tool suggest that such activity is necessary to *Radical Awakening*, nor does it judge whatever perspective feels comfortable to the reader.

We also wish to emphasize that all prayers have their place. They can range from the most ordinary level, such as, "Oh God, please let my team win the game," to the more complex and complicated, such as, "Oh God, please let me survive this medical diagnosis so that I may be here to raise my children." Here, it's important to note how quick the mind is to judge one prayer as "frivolous" and the other as "valid," but Pure Consciousness includes All That Is, and rejects *nothing*. It is worth repeating that the Universe itself has no judgment about such matters. Only the mind judges and classifies things as "more" or "less" valuable.

The Many Contexts of Prayer

Although prayer is often a spontaneous expression of a desire to change some situation, be it large or small, it may be helpful to explore other possible contexts for prayer. The mind's hope is often to generate some form of relief from current conditions, whether those conditions are our own, or someone else's.

In some cases, prayer happens when we feel we have nowhere else to turn. At that point, our instinctual urge is to reach out to something beyond ourselves– to some higher power, to some benevolent being, to some god or goddess. The Bible, for example, defines *faith* as "the assurance of things hoped for, the conviction of things not seen..." (Hebrews 11:1). In this sense, prayer is largely an expression of optimism that some intelligent or benevolent being, somewhere *out there*, will intervene in our time of need.

Seen differently, it can also involve a humbling act of surrender. For some, this can be a new experience. The human tendency is to believe that there's virtually nothing humanity cannot fix. Of course, there's evidence all around us that this isn't so. But, for some of us, it's only when we face a life-altering event, one which we can't control or change, that we succumb to prayer.

Real surrender is what enables prayer to work. When we let go into the Formless, we open the pathway for change, one marked by the absence of ego. Transformations, and even "miracles," can occur when a new space is created within. Even if the answer to the prayer doesn't come in the time or form we'd hoped for, this doesn't mean it was "useless." We need only make one small step or gesture towards the Divine, and the Divine will move exponentially toward us. Many great teachers across all boundaries of time, geography, religions and cultures advocate this truism. In the words of the Indian saint, Sri Mata Amritanandamayi Devi, *"If we take one step towards Goddess, Goddess will take the other 99 steps towards us."*

Instructions for the Prayer Tool

This tool requires some devotion to the practice. It can become a powerful tool on our "tool belt," one that can last a lifetime. As Sri Ramana Maharshi says, *"Place your burden at the feet of the Lord of the universe who is ever victorious and accomplishes everything. Abide in the heart and surrender your acts to the Divine."*

There can also be a final stage beyond prayer itself. Here, we can move into a space of total acceptance of what is, or whatever will be. At this point, the desire for change falls away altogether, leaving us in an enlightened state in which one knows that *everything is, as it is*.

The Universe and every action or inaction within it unfold without the mind or ego's intervention. Life flows naturally, with no desire for a particular shift or outcome. In reaching this condition, not only does this tool become obsolete, but the "tool belt" itself becomes obsolete as well. With Grace, our response to life's unfolding can evolve beyond our imagining.

Sri Ramana Maharshi was also clear about this stage beyond prayer:

"Give up all sense of 'I' and 'mine' and leave it to the Lord to do what He likes with you. Surrender can never be regarded as complete so long as the devotee wants this or that from the Lord. True surrender is the love of God for the sake of love and nothing else."

CHAPTER 7
The Inner Spiritual Director: Your Best Advisor and Most Dangerous Enemy

What if all your sincere effort to be a better person, to live a more spiritual life, and to be a more loving person, was the *very thing* complicating your existence and leading you to suffer? We may immediately wonder, "How could this be possible? These efforts are the things that give life meaning, and encourage me to actualize my full spiritual and human potential? How could this be complicating my life?"

Although these efforts are useful at one level, their less obvious qualities are what trip us up. For example, at their root, these efforts can contain desires and hidden agendas of the *I-thought*. Being aware of these dynamics helps us to unmask the false identity of these thoughts and agendas: I call it, the "Inner Spiritual Director," or the ISD.

The Inner Spiritual Director has probably been there all along and has perhaps even helped prepare us for our Awakening. We may even recognize the ISD as having been, at one point, a genuine friend and guide during the time leading up to this shift. It might have shown up as a quiet whisper in our ear, encouraging us to keep seeking spiritual truths, to learn more about ourselves, and to go within.

This Director may have witnessed a brief glimpse of an Awakening within us, or encouraged us to listen more carefully to something that hit a mystical chord in our soul. The ISD inspired us to start down the path of spiritual authenticity.

At this initial stage, the Inner Spiritual Director does us a great service. We don't mean to *disparage* this part of ourselves, a part that watches out for us at the beginning of the journey, and heartens us not to give up the quest. At first, it uses whatever methods it can to keep us moving deeper and closer to Consciousness. The ISD, however, is always playing a role. Early on, it disguises itself as a caring advisor who wants to guide us; ironically, it's successful in playing this part, *at the beginning*. In this way, the ISD works to our advantage. <u>But, underneath its spiritual robes, is the ego.</u> In this new stage of Awakening, the ISD's more selfish intentions become a major stumbling block to our deepening into Consciousness.

The *I-thought* finds this newfound awareness to be threatening to all that it has worked hard to create. It would not be overreaching to say that the *I-thought* interprets our Awakening as a menace to its very existence. And, in one sense, this is true. When we perceive ourselves as unified with All That Is, no longer as a separate self, this newfound Awakening *does* put an end to the solidity and authority of the *I-thought*.

The ego's prime agenda is maintaining its dominance. Nothing could be more frightening to an ego than the thought of its own disappearance. If we recall our Radical Awakening experience, we might even have sensed a feeling of "disappearing" in connection with our feelings of expansiveness. That moment is the very instant when the separate *I-thought* dissolves, and we recognize our True nature as being One with All That Is.

Emerging from a Radical Awakening session, then, the newly refined Awareness is useful in detecting the presence of the ISD. This Awareness raises the attentiveness needed to detect the mind's subtlest patterns. We begin to recognize the early warning signs of its presence. These are the triggers that propel us onto an unproductive path. Holding the Inner Spiritual Director up to the light exposes it for what it truly is: a skillful trickster. Moreover, being aware of its dynamics helps us to unmask its false identity.

The Deceptive Nature of the Inner Spiritual Director

We see that the ISD operates as an extension of the ego. When reduced to its most basic parts, the ego's actions are quite simple: If things are going the way the ego wants them to go, the ego is happy. When it is satisfied, it gives directions– via our busy minds– as to how we can sustain that happiness. To increase its bottomless desire for happiness, the ISD boosts one's self-importance with more impressive and fascinating spiritual experiences.

When things are not conforming to the ego's expectations, it is unhappy. When it is unhappy, it directs us to manage the people and things around us, so we are more likely to get what we want. The ISD, in its newly assumed identity, mimics a variety of spiritual actions and behaviors, previously collected by the ego from many contexts. In reality, the ISD is merely wrapped up in a new *spiritual façade*.

The cleverness of this tactic is that it enables us to fall back into misidentification with a separate sense of self. In other words, the *I-thought* co-opts the Awakening so that it can continue to exist undetected. Once truly experienced, however, the Awakening cannot be undone. *Radical Awakening* pulls back the curtain on the "Great and Powerful Oz," the *I-thought*, and things can never truly be the same. No matter how strong the pull of the outside world, we can never fully return to our old, conditioned ways of being and thinking.

A friend once spoke to me about an Awakening that was co-opted in this way by the ISD. For quite some time, her perception of reality had no longer moved according to outer circumstances.

"Everything was the same Pure Consciousness, looking back at itself. The stability remained, whether I was asleep, awake, doing the dishes, or walking the dog...no difference. I still experienced a full range of emotions, but there was always a Knowing that a deeper reality existed beneath. And this lasted for weeks and weeks.

Then, one day, the man I'd been dating for over a year told me that, if I didn't finish filing the paperwork for my divorce *immediately*, he would lose custody of his five-year-old daughter forever. He claimed that the mother of his child would have her wealthy attorneys depict him as morally unfit to care for the child because he was dating a 'married woman.'

His words devastated me. My ex and I had been moving through our divorce peacefully, and our timetable was never of consequence to either of us. When I thought that I could single-handedly cause this man to lose his custody case and potentially ruin his visitation rights with his little girl– I was overwhelmed and humiliated. Certainly, I was not an Awakened, compassionate, spiritual being if I caused so much distress. I went straight into a state of shame and urgency. And just like that, what had seemed so obvious and so constant for the past several weeks vanished. I felt torn down, both emotionally and spiritually, in the worst ways imaginable."

The Inner Spiritual Director's conclusions led my friend to hurtful thoughts about herself, and even about the veracity of her Awakening. Its judgments about the world and her situation were harsh, even to the point of skillfully making her question the Awakening itself. Although this emotionally and ethically charged situation ultimately deepened her awareness of Pure Consciousness, this anecdote illustrates that, as much of a "friend" as the ISD can be early on during our journey, a darker side can emerge when it feels sidelined and no longer relevant.

Continuing the Search

Another way the ISD maintains its relevancy is to keep us revved up on the path to Awakening. Rather than tearing us down at one of the crossroads, it continues to coax us forward by suggesting that what we've experienced isn't a *true* Awakening. It applauds the moment while adding the phrase, "...so far." "What you experienced was amazing– so far." "You've reached a great turning point– so far." It eagerly whispers that there's still more to learn, more to experience, more to achieve. This pattern is especially subtle because so many of us have already been participating in self-help and spiritual growth activities for a long time. By now, we are deep in the habit of searching.

The desire to keep seeking *after* our Radical Awakening, though, is a trap. This is why Papaji is known for his instruction, "*Call off the search.*" The method to halt this activity is often called, "Self-Inquiry." Just asking the question, "Where is the '*I*' who needs to be awakened again?" can provide an instant reflection back to Who We Really Are. It is this inquiry that decommissions the (mis)identification with the "I." This inquiry is precisely what makes Step 6 such a powerful tool. When this occurs, we are back in touch with our Inner Truth, which then guides us home.

Another friend acknowledged to me that she had become a "spiritual growth junkie," going on retreat after retreat. When she had an Awakening experience, she barely recognized it, because her mind discounted it so quickly. So, she continued attending these events, even after her awakening, having become "hooked" on spiritual growth activities.

There was always someone telling her about the wondrous message of yet another spiritual master. Or, she would hear about a weekend retreat in a location with special spiritual energies. Or, she would buy a new set of audio recordings with special tones or mantras that promised to take her to continuous bliss.

After spending a lot of money and time, she finally recognized the hook, "Maybe if I do this I'll be truly enlightened because I'll constantly be in bliss." What she found after a Radical Awakening session with me was that her Awakening had not gone away; there had just been clouds obscuring it. Most of the clouds were coming from her own mind, telling her that she hadn't had a *real* Awakening, and needed more *experiences* to get her to that point. This doubt was like an infection that kept eating away at her sense of True Self.

Now, she still goes to an occasional event, "But I end up where I'm supposed to be because my feet just take me there." Moreover, she says she learns from them and enjoys them: "I go because they are *reminders* of who I Really Am. Sometimes, I go because I like the sense of community. I like the teacher and other participants and enjoy the camaraderie. I still have the pull to fix myself more, but I see it and examine it for what it is, the *Trap of Doubt*."

Giving Power to the "I"

As a person opens their spiritual Consciousness to a higher level, it's possible that extraordinary gifts will appear. For example, some expensive tickets to a sold-out concert are suddenly freely given to you by a stranger. In such cases, the personal sense of "*I*" can become inflated, because the person believes the gifts are theirs. The person doesn't realize that what has happened is an opening to a glimpse of the Divine. Such gifts are signs that there is a vast, unseen space beyond our physical mind and body that encompasses us, and everything else that we can fathom. It is from this realm that all is created.

If we are not aware of how the ISD gives power to the *I-thought*, these gifts can give the impression that, "I am creating my reality because I am such a good meditator." To recall our earlier discussions, the *I-thought* leads us to identify with the body/mind, or the personality. By not realizing that we are empowering the *I-thought* when we take ownership of such gifts, we move away from the True Self, rather than towards it.

One insidious aspect of the ISD is how subtly it hides its true intentions. To a person on a spiritual or self-improvement path, the ISD almost always operates without being noticed. As mentioned above, its behavior can even co-opt our awakening to the True Self. Without vigilance, it can make itself the center of the newly discovered Self. It will even take credit for creating the new "us." It hastily overlooks who or what else has contributed to its successes, unappreciative of the Grace that is running through its life.

Being the Judge and the Jury

Another clue to watch for is evidence of compulsive attraction or aversion to things, experiences, or people. The Buddhists refer to this pattern of behavior as *grasping* or *avoidance*. I'm not speaking here of valid desires to take care of ourselves by doing certain things to remain healthy, or avoiding things that adversely affect our well-being. I refer to those base desires and fears that can be covered over with spiritual justification.

The Inner Spiritual Director is usually involved in these strong emotional responses. It tells us that we are justified in having these feelings, often giving a list of unsubstantiated reasons. The ISD presents the reasons as "true," when it is only supporting its position according to various logical fallacies.

One judgment favored by the ISD is the setting of *Rules of Behavior for Spiritual People*. A short list of such behaviors might include the following: dietary restrictions; an exact number of hours spent in daily meditation; a regular yoga practice; humility; no smoking; no drugs; total celibacy; or a compulsion to point out the spiritual failings of those around us so that they can "grow," for example.

The spiritual person is then easily categorized as being "more" or "less" spiritual--usually by other "more" or "less" spiritual people. If all of those rules were true, non-compliance with the *spiritually approved list* would probably eliminate a great number of enlightened beings who have graced our planet. Our preconceptions of what is spiritually "right" and "wrong" are often based on egoic judgments, rather than on spiritual reality.

I don't condone inappropriate behavior, of course. But we need to check if we're being objective or judgmental. When acting objectively, we view a situation carefully to discriminate between right and wrong action. We know we are behaving inappropriately judgmental when there is an emotional charge surrounding the situation. With observant action, we look at the facts from a place of love and understanding, then make a decision about how to respond.

When we practice being undisturbed by the ISD, it can be put back to work in its proper place. Now, we are more selective about its advice, because our shift has produced new vision. We have gained discernment. The ISD may continue to give us directions, but they are now options to look at and consider, rather than imperatives to follow.

After your *Radical Awakening*, you can contact your own True Inner Knowing, which reveals directly which options are worthwhile for you to follow, and which are not. From this space, we can act in a manner that leads to unassuming behavior, genuine harmony, and true peace.

CHAPTER 8
A Tale of Two Seekers

*J*t was 1996, and I was settling in for the flight from San Francisco to Lucknow, India. I was flying economy class, and as I looked at the seat next to mine. I had to smile. I wondered if the airline allows a person to buy two adjacent seats, one for me and the other for my fallen ego.

This was my second trip to Lucknow. The first time, a year earlier, I had no money problems. I had co-founded the Transpersonal Hypnotherapy Institute in Boulder, Colorado, which my partner and I built to be one of the top transpersonal training centers in the country. I was living in a 5,600 square-foot, custom home in the Rockies, which was backed up against 90,000 acres of national forest. I spent two months a year in each of the locations of Sedona, Hawaii, Northern Californian and the Colorado Rockies – places I carefully chose, as I loved each of them for their beauty and power. I hiked in beautiful red-rock canyons, went scuba diving and windsurfed in aqua-green pristine oceans, rock climbed in premiere climbing areas in Thailand, and skied world-class powder – all while teaching and developing work that I loved.

I heard about this man in India, H. W. L. Poonja, or Papaji as he was called by his devotees. A few of my friends and colleagues had been with Papaji, and they were lit up when they returned to the States.

I had also seen a video about him and sensed that he was the real deal, a spiritual Master. I had started on the spiritual path when I was sixteen and had devoted my life to the goal of spiritual awakening. I was thinking, "I've done so many years of study and practice and been blessed with good teachers. I taught my first meditation class in 1970 after studying with Zen Master Suzuki Roshi. I somehow mused, in my state of ego inflation, that I was probably pretty close to enlightenment.

I heard people say that Papaji could wake people up. "He could give me the last little push I need," I thought to myself. I got on a plane and traveled to India. Little did I realize that the extra seat I needed on that first flight was for my arrogance and ego. I was full of myself.

My first impression of Papaji was how kind and charismatic he was. After some time, I also sensed a peace in his presence and how meditation became easy and natural.

In retrospect, I should have spent more time getting my sea legs under me, being with him and hearing what he was saying. I listened to what he said but I wasn't *hearing* him. He would often say, "No practices; practices reinforce the doer, which will just get you into trouble." What was that about? I'm thinking, "Come on, let's get down to business. Give me the little push."

Eventually I had the opportunity to ask Papaji a question. I asked him what I had to let go of in order to become enlightened. The question seemed pretty reasonable to me.

Papaji responded, "Okay, well let's check out your attachments. I will ask you about some attachments, and you will tell me about them."

He asked me about my attachment to work, to money and to women. The first two parts of my life were clicking along, and though I had just ended a ten-year relationship with the lady who was my partner at the Transpersonal Hypnotherapy Institute, we seemed to have parted amicably and I was feeling free and enjoying it. I answered in what seemed a reasonable way. I told him I had no attachments to these things.

Then Papaji asked, "What about attachment to freedom?"

I wanted to give him the right answer. If I had been truthful to myself, I would have said, "I don't have attachment to freedom. If I have freedom, it's good, and if I don't, it's fine. I just thought that I would ask." But I remembered how Ram Das said that the desire for freedom is the final desire to go before enlightenment. Since I saw myself as close to enlightenment, the desire for freedom would nicely fill out my résumé, that my slate was clean except for the final desire for freedom.

I said, "Yes Papa, I am attached to freedom."

He replied, "Okay, this is good. So you have an attachment to freedom, and this is what you have to let go of, then you will be free."

I thought, "Fine," and that was the end of our interaction.

Amazingly, the next day I woke up and every description I had read of enlightenment I was living. There was the moment-to-moment feeling of great peace and a sense of knowing the True Self deeply, feeling just solid in it.

I was living in a world of magic as well. Every thought I had materialized or appeared instantly in some reflection of my surrounding circumstances. I remember going to *satsang* that morning, and as I was riding my bicycle, I had the feeling my past was totally over.

Everything about Yukio was over. I looked over at the buildings I was passing, and amongst the many with Hindi and Punjabi names was "Mount Eden Trust." I could hardly believe it because Mount Eden is the area in San Francisco where I lived as a young child.

I began reading esoteric texts like the *Ribhu Gita*. I had read them before but found them heady. Now I was reading them and they were my soul being sung. There was such a feeling of love and connectedness, day after day – for two weeks. Occasionally there would be a thought floating by: "I did it. I let go of my attachment to freedom, and that was the final push I needed. I am living enlightened, as fully realized consciousness."

The day before I was to return to the West, enlightenment, realized consciousness – the whole thing – stopped cold. It was over. There wasn't even a trace. It was as if it had never happened. I had a memory of it but couldn't contact a thing. I picked up the *Ribhu Gita* and it was like trying to read a book on calculus. I freaked out.

What followed was basically me doing myself in with my self-possession. It reminds me of the line in *The Shawshank Redemption*: "How can you be so obtuse?" I wrote Papaji a letter telling him what had happened. But did I express any gratitude to him for the gift he had given me? No, I actually demanded that he help me get it back.

Papaji responded by writing right on my note: "<u>BAD LUCK</u>!" Beneath that he wrote: "Don't know if it is going to come back. In fact, I don't even know if it is going to come back in this lifetime or even in your next lifetime. Your next lifetime may not even be human, maybe an insect."

My response to this was adolescent collapse. It was as if I were a whiny teenage girl who's been grounded, and then the father says, "For the next year your diet is bread and water. When you have memorized the telephone book, then maybe you can go on a date."

Actually, I do a disservice to teenage girls because no girl would believe the father; he's just yanking her chain. But I believed Papaji. Oh yeah, he had condemned me to spiritual purgatory, and because of my pitiful destiny didn't I have the right to be angry? You bet. I became possessed with righteous anger.

Several people close to Papaji tried to get me to cool off and stay. They told me that they had occasionally seen him work this way with hard cases, and when the person hung in and got the lesson, there was both real growth and real gratitude.

I remember in particular how one man said, "Papaji is very impatient with people who don't listen to him. What was his instruction to you? His instruction was to let go of your attachment to freedom. And here you have written three pages crying about how you lost it, and demonstrating to him all of your attachment to freedom.

That is directly the opposite of what he told you to do." They all reminded me how from the beginning Papaji had told me to stay until I was "well cooked" and I had agreed. They said his letter was an invitation to stay and receive his grace.

I wasn't having any of it. The only thing I could hear was the voice in my head hammering: "This is all bullshit. What kind of teacher is he anyway to give me this thing and take it away like this? I am leaving and I am never coming back. There is nothing here for me. Who needs this? I have enough to get through my life. I can just do it without him."

The above probably sounds like a bad B movie, but the pain of it was very real. It put me on my knees, and I was forced into deep introspection and self-analysis. I recognized that the things I had told Papaji I wasn't attached to, now I was suffering the loss of. Not being attached to them was easy when I had them, but when I didn't, it wasn't so easy. I had been attached to them all along.

I saw my hubris: how I'd thought I was close to enlightenment and just needed a little push to get me there. Now I remembered the biographies I'd read of great Realizers and the discipline they had and their burning desire for liberation, of their unwavering faith in their Guru. Did I have those qualities? All it took was a note from Papaji with a few lines of scathing criticism and I'd rejected him.

In my soul searching, one thing became strikingly clear: I needed more than anything to establish a spiritual center that would be unwavering amidst the conditions of life in the world. I realized that as long as my primary identification was as a separate person entangled in desire and fear, attached to the outcome of my actions, I could never be free. I knew that I must awaken for freedom to happen.

I remembered what Papaji had said: "If your desire for freedom is true, your freedom is guaranteed." I saw for the first time in my thirty years of spiritual practice what that statement really meant: I needed my spiritual center more than my next breath.

Then I had a dream. I was in a room and a huge sixty-foot *Nataraja*, the dancing Shiva, the Hindu God of destruction, was coming after me while a drum was playing. Every time the drum played, he would move towards me. I tried to escape from the room, but it had no doors and no windows; there was no place for me to go. Then I looked over to the corner of the room and saw Papaji playing the drum.

The next day I called my best friend, Bob, who was a long-time devotee of the American spiritual teacher Adi Da. Bob and I used to have arguments about Gurus because I wasn't into teachers.

When I told him about the dream, he said, "Isn't it obvious?"

I replied, "Well, no."

"He is your teacher, and he is orchestrating this whole thing. *Nataraja* coming after you is just this stripping you of everything. Well, now there is no escape, and the only thing you can do is to go back to him."

The light went on, and I thought, "That is totally true."

But I had no money; I didn't even have the money to buy a ticket. The money had gone to wild living with my girlfriend, furnishing our house and then all the attorney fees. So I did a renegade transpersonal training.

I decided right then to go back to India, but this time I was returning with my head in my hand. The little butt kicking life had laid on me gave me the essential gift I brought to Papaji: humility. And this time I was staying till I was well cooked.

Papaji loved to tell the story of meeting his Master, Ramana Maharishi. Papa had come to Ramana to find God. Somewhat like me he had heard that this man could show him God, and also, like me, he had come for the experience of God, or what he imagined would be a permanent experience of God.

In fact, much like me, he even had a certain arrogance in his first encounters with Ramana. However, unlike me, when he told Ramana he wanted to see God, he meant it. You see, there are a couple of qualities that can "get you through the door" when you approach a Master: complete humility and the burning desire to know God. Papaji had the second.

I first heard about Papaji from some of my colleagues; Papaji heard about Ramana Maharshi in a very different way. It was 1944 and Papaji had just completed a two-year journey throughout India seeking a teacher who could show him God.

Throughout his life, from the time he was a boy, Papaji was in love with Krishna, and he was often blessed with visions of him. Many nights they would dance together in ecstasy.

In Hinduism devotion to a deity is called *bhakti*, and a spiritual aspirant, or *bhakta*, can devote his life to attaining even a single vision of his chosen deity. It is a measure of Papaji's maturity that he enjoyed intimacy with Krishna throughout his life.

Over time Papaji began to experience a dilemma: although he enjoyed ecstatic meetings with Krishna, he had to admit that Krishna did not always appear to him, and too, after each encounter he experienced something of a letdown. The bliss of the experience was not permanent. In Lucknow Papaji used the analogy of chocolate. He said he had tasted chocolate but he wanted to taste chocolate all the time. Thus he sought a teacher who could make the bliss permanent.

Papaji's search was urgent. He abandoned his promising military career and left his wife and children in the care of his parents at their home in the Punjab. He had the firm conviction that a teacher, a Master, should be able to give him the permanent experience of God, and he made clear to any teacher he approached that he would give anything, even his life, if they would do so. But he was not willing to wait; he expected the teacher to deliver the goods.

Papaji said he met many sincere teachers in different ashrams, and each promised that if he stayed and did *sadhana* (spiritual practice) according to their instructions, then he would experience God. Papaji was not satisfied with this answer, and he found it especially dubious when he saw old men with long white beards who had done *sadhana* their whole lives in an ashram and had yet to realize God. Dejected, he eventually returned home.

One day shortly after his return, he was sitting in his parents' house, at a loss for what to do next, when there was a knock on the door. He opened the door and a *sadhu* stood before him.

Papaji invited the *sadhu* in and fed him. He decided to give it another try and asked him if he knew anyone who could show him God. To his surprise, the *sadhu* responded that Ramana Maharshi could show him God. He told him that Ramana lived in Tiruvannamalai, South India about one hundred miles from Madras. He even drew a map of how to get to his ashram.

Papaji was intrigued by what the *sadhu* told him, but he was unemployed, without a rupee to his name. Not only that, his father had made clear that he'd had just about enough of his peripatetic son and his search for God. It was time for him to get a job and support his family.

Papa left the house and walked along a street to a local tea shop. The owner recognized him and said, "Harwal, I hear you are no longer in the army." He sensed Papa's situation and said, "Here, let me give you a *chai*."

Papa sat down and began to drink his *chai*, when he noticed a newspaper. He picked it up and scanned the want ads. There it was: "Wanted ex-military officer to run commissary in Madras." Within a short time Papaji had landed the job and arrived in Madras. He had two weeks before the job started, and he immediately set off to meet Ramana Maharshi.

When Papa arrived at Ramana Ashram, he walked to the hall where Ramana gave *darshan*. *Darshan* means "sight" or "vision," and it refers to the meeting of a devotee with a holy person. When Papaji entered, Ramana was reclining on his sofa as different people passed before him in respect and gratitude, with their hands folded in *namaste*. Papaji had a completely different reaction: he took one look at Ramana and became furious.

Papa saw that before him was the very same *sadhu* who had told him about Ramana Maharshi at his home in the Punjab. He felt duped that he had been lured all the way to Tiruvannamalai. He started towards Ramana, yelling, "You are an imposter. How could you trick me, pretending you were a *sadhu* when you were only sending me to you?" He actually had to be physically restrained by two of Ramana's attendants. Then he turned and walked out of the hall.

Luckily, as he was leaving the ashram, another man approached him. He recognized that Papa was North Indian and asked why he was leaving so quickly when clearly, he must have travelled a long way to see Ramana.

Papaji heatedly explained how Ramana had appeared to him in the Punjab and if he were genuine, he could have answered his questions then and there. He said Ramana was just another fake swami interested in ensnaring followers any way he could.

The man told him that Ramana had not left Tiruvannamalai in fifty years. He also told him that this type of phenomenon had happened before, that an American lady had even met Ramana in Florida where he told her to come to Tiruvannamalai.

Papaji was intrigued, and he decided to approach Ramana and ask him a couple of questions. He asked if he was the same *sadhu* who had come to his house in the Punjab. Ramana remained silent. Then he asked if he could show him God.

Ramana replied that he could not show him God and no one else could either, because God is not an object to be seen but the seer. He should not concern himself with objects that can be seen, but find out who the seer is.

Papa was annoyed by Ramana's answer. It was as if he were telling him to be chocolate rather than taste it, and for a Krishna *bhakta* this holds little appeal. Before he could dismiss the advice, however, Ramana gave him a remarkable spiritual experience, one he had never had before.

At times in Lucknow Papaji tried to find words to describe the experience, though he was never completely satisfied with his efforts. He said that Ramana opened his heart, though it was not the physical heart or the heart *chakra*.

It was the heart of pure consciousness, and yet it also had a subtle, beautiful form. The experience thrilled Papaji and gave him his first begrudging respect for Ramana.

Papaji was a hard nut to crack because the next time he talked to Ramana he approached him as if he was boasting. It was about a week after the first encounter, and Ramana asked him where he had been. He replied that he had been spending time on Arunachala playing with Krishna.

Papaji expected his answer would give Ramana pause because he was sure Ramana had not had such experiences himself. Instead Ramana asked if he saw Krishna now, and Papa admitted that he did not. Ramana said "What appears and disappears is not real." This answer further annoyed Papa; his experiences were seemingly being dismissed out of hand.

Papaji's third meeting with Ramana changed his relation to him completely. During this visit a group of Krishna *bhaktas* who were on a pilgrimage passing through Tiruvannamalai came to Ramana for his blessing. One of them had a small painting of Krishna, which he showed Ramana.

Papaji could see the painting and that it was an especially beautiful portrait. Then he saw tears in Ramana's eyes, and at the same time he felt a wave of love flowing from him that was as powerful as any he had ever experienced.

Papaji was astonished: this man was really a great *bhakta;* he only hid his devotion behind his advice about finding the seer. From that moment on he had complete faith in Ramana.

The end of Papaji's seeking took place during his fourth encounter with Ramana. This time he came to ask him about an unusual situation he found himself in. For some time he had been concentrating almost every waking moment on repeating a devotional *mantra* to Krishna, but suddenly he could no longer do so.

For some inexplicable reason his mind refused to repeat the *mantra*, even a single time. For a Krishna *bhakta* this was a serious problem. When Papa explained the situation, Ramana first showed him how his entire life of spiritual practice had served its purpose and that there was nothing more to do.

Then he told him that the movement of awareness, which seeks for something outside itself, should look back and recognize its real nature. This time Papa was ripe for Ramana's advice, and with the force of Ramana's spiritual transmission facilitating the process, he directly experienced the true Seer. He instantly recognized that the Seer was who he is, this is his very Self, the God he has been seeking.

Unlike his visions of Krishna, *this* was not an experience. The Self, consciousness itself, never loses its self-nature, no matter what may arise in the field of perception. It is at rest prior to seeking, the unchanging condition of body, mind and world.

Papaji now knew that the freedom he had been searching for all his life is the inherent, natural state of the True Seer, or pure consciousness.

His search for an ongoing spiritual experience ended when he finally discovered that which does not appear and disappear.

When Papa told the story of his time with Ramana, it was very difficult not to be overcome by the emotion involved. He told it with the most amazing mix of self-effacing humor and heart-breaking gratitude. I remember one time in particular when his words had a profound effect on me.

When Ramana said to Papaji, "What appears and disappears is not real;" it was as if I were right there with him. When he explained that awareness is moving into the realm of experience, and that every experience must come and go, I realized I had never really considered this for myself. It was as if I were hearing it for the first time, and I immediately wondered what could exist beyond the realm of experience.

I followed Ramana's guidance to look back to find out who is the seer, and at first, I didn't see anything. But then it opened up for me. I found myself face to face with an infinite, conscious awareness, the same awareness I had first contacted when I had looked into Papaji's right eye, as described in the Preface of this book.

Now I saw how this awareness is always at peace, regardless of the situations in my life. Somehow, I also understood that this was more than just another "aha" moment. I knew, from the core of my being, that this awareness is my very self and it is always present.

I remembered how Papaji would use the words "true knowledge," or just "knowing," and I had not understood what he was saying. Now I did. True knowledge is the certainty of who I am. It is beyond experience or intellectual understanding; it is inherent in consciousness itself; the self-nature of consciousness is recognized as my self-nature too.

The words of Andrew Cohen, a former student of Papaji, in my first *satsang* with him, came to me: "Maturation into True Realization does not lie in how many blissful experiences of oneness you have, but in deepening the foundation of true knowing."

Papaji said that when he approached Ramana to ask him his first questions, he was aware that he was in the presence of immense silence. He felt the same silence from the mountain Arunachala.

Though he would resist Ramana's advice, he knew that Ramana and the mountain were something special. Similarly, I felt the peace that surrounded Papaji. And though I would resist Papaji and even reject him at first, I knew that somehow in his presence the transformation I desperately wanted could occur.

Not long after the certainty of who I am was revealed to me, Papaji gave me my spiritual name, Ramana. A few days later I and a small group of others were eating lunch with him at his home. He said that some people were having trouble with self-enquiry.

He asked me if I could help them. I said of course, I would do what I could. He pointed to several people and asked them to work with me. The origin of Radical Awakening was my agreement to help others with self-enquiry.

I was quickly struck by the challenge I had undertaken. Self-enquiry is the technique Ramana Maharshi recommended to those who came to him. It investigates thinking and specifically the root thought – "I." Ramana would ask people to enquire, "Who is this 'I'?" or "From whence does it arise?"

The practice sounds straightforward, but as anyone who has seriously undertaken it can tell you, it can be very challenging. Indeed, I had diligently tried it myself and had struck out completely. I just got nowhere. So what was I doing agreeing to teach something I hadn't mastered myself? In fact, my first thought was: "What am I to do with these people?"

I remembered the peace that surrounded Papaji. I had been watching him work with others for more than a hundred *satsangs*, and I saw how he had a unique way of getting people to notice the peace and then establish them in it. Like that, I reasoned that if those who came to me could somehow become aware of a greater dimension of themselves, then self-enquiry from that space should be easier.

An important part of my work in the beginning was considering space and awareness. I noticed that when I contemplated space it had a magical quality. When I became aware of it, it became filled with awareness; it was not just empty.

Awareness of space became the space of awareness. I decided to start by having people notice the space around them and then the stillness in that space. This became the first step of Radical Awakening. Almost like magic it worked. People told me they felt a seamless, peaceful quality and how they relaxed into it.

I remembered the *satsang* with Papaji when I had followed Ramana's guidance to look back and find out who is the seer. I wanted this to come alive for others as it had for me. I knew it should occur within the expanded sense of space created by the first step.

I had to lay additional groundwork for this to happen, and as a model I used one of the changes that had occurred in my sensorium after my own awakening. The biggest change was the sense of sight, and incorporating this change enabled me to create steps two through four.

There was a touch of serendipity to the whole thing because the critical advice to look back and find the Seer, which became step five, was now intimately connected with the sense of sight. The guidance to look back, though dealing with awareness, a somewhat abstract instruction, was no longer abstract. The person was actually able to look and, most importantly, to see.

I had to be very careful with the use of language, and in doing so I discovered something wonderful: how certain words such as awareness, consciousness, the True Seer, which are usually very difficult to grasp, have real power when introduced at the right moment in steps four and five. They come alive.

Step six is the fruition of all I had intuited: yes, self-enquiry becomes much easier when practiced from the expanded sense of self.

This book is an invitation to become part of what I was given by my teacher. My time with Papaji was a continuing revelation of the wisdom of a man who *knew*.

In order to see this, to stop doubting and pay attention, I had to be humbled. When Papaji asked me to work with people, I think he sensed there is another way: that if his teaching could be presented in a practical way, by a westerner to westerners, it would have a receptive audience. He said that westerners were an enigma to him.

He was fascinated by how they were actually interested in the highest teaching he had to offer. They wanted freedom. Very few of his Indian devotees wanted that. They came to Papa simply because they loved him.

He said that Indians, or at least some Indians, had the purity that made their approach fruitful. If you loved him, he would do the rest. Westerners are not like that; they have to be shown and their skepticism overcome.

Papa never assumed any fundamental limitation in those who came to him. How could he? He was there to show others their very nature, how his state was in truth their state, too. If there were some stumbling blocks, he just hadn't found the way to communicate what he had to offer. I think that Papa's attitude is the key to this book. He was a spiritual scientist, without preconceptions or prejudice. When you read this book, have that same attitude.

Ramana Maharshi was often asked about the means to Realization. His Teaching, or his philosophical understanding of man and the world, was not unique. It was essentially the understanding contained in *Advaita Vedanta*, the highest knowledge of the Vedas, the oldest Hindu scriptures.

Advaita Vedanta teaches that there is one unchanging Reality, or consciousness itself, which is the substratum of all that exists. It is the Reality of the world and also of everything that arises subjectively such as mind and emotions. When this Reality is fully realized, it is known to be one's true identity, the Self.

People came to Ramana from all walks of life, and they spanned the complete spectrum of spiritual practice. Most of them were interested in the means to Realization; they were not so interested in the Teaching as the way to realize the Teaching.

The way he taught is generally understood to be self-enquiry. Here he was unique. Though it is possible to find some parallels to this technique in Hindu scriptures, it had never been explained as precisely as he did. At times he said that self-enquiry is the one, infallible way to Realization.

However, at times Ramana also talked about the way of *bhakti*. He spoke of it with such high regard, that it is fair to say he put it on equal footing with self-enquiry. Indeed, he himself exhibited displays of *bhakti* that would leave those around him speechless.

Ramana liked to recount stories from classical devotional literature, especially those of great devotees and the incidents in their lives where their love of God and Guru demonstrated the heights of *bhakti*.

When he recounted these stories, he would enact each of the characters as a master actor would, and the poetry that came from his lips would go straight to the heart of the listener. But then he would stop. There would be tears streaming from his eyes. When he recovered, he said that he simply could not continue, and he didn't know how anyone could tell these stories without being overcome by the *bhakti* in them.

I had never experienced this type of *bhakti* until I came to Papaji. I really couldn't understand it. But after my awakening I did experience it, and I also discovered a beautiful similarity between my life and Papaji's. I think that what follows is a perfect way to end this story of two seekers. It is taken from an interview I did with Chris Boys in Tiruvannamalai:

Chris: I know that there was a time in Lucknow where you experienced great gratitude and love for Papaji. Talk about that.

Ramana: There were some ladies who used to go to Papaji's house everyday and stand outside and look through a window at him in the morning. One morning, I found myself going to join them. I couldn't help myself. I just never wanted to take my eyes off of him. I did this every day for weeks, and I actually began to feel like a teenage girl in love. Occasionally I would experience a bit of doubt, because I had never had feelings like that for a man. But it didn't matter; just to see him was overwhelming and I let it happen.

Chris: You know, something similar took place between Papaji and Ramana.

Ramana: It did?

Chris: Yes, after Papaji's enlightenment he was so in love with Ramana that he too never wanted to take his eyes off of him. In the ashram from noon till about two o'clock Ramana was left alone in the *darshan* hall. But Papaji found a crack in one of the walls where he could see Ramana's couch, and he would stand there the whole time. He said that he couldn't see his Master, except just occasionally Ramana would move his arm in such a way that he would catch a glimpse of it, and that was enough.

Papaji also spoke with great approval of the poet Muruganar because he too never took his eyes off of Ramana and then he wrote thousands of poems in praise of his Master.

Ramana: What you are saying is really affecting me, because when I went up to receive my name from Papaji I first recited to him a poem by Muruganar. Papaji had my new name written on a slip of paper, but after I recited the poem he changed it and gave me the name Ramana.

Chris: David Godman has said that from all his research he has concluded that self-enquiry was not the primary teaching of Ramana Maharshi; it was love.

Ramana: Yes, that is the where the great physics of the universe is found. It is in a love relationship.

CHAPTER 9
The Tree of Awareness

There is a level in Consciousness that exists deeper than the level of experience. In Hinduism this is referred to as True Knowing or True Knowledge. Ramana Maharshi simply referred to it as the Heart. The Heart is the center that we never leave, even though we have the experience that we do. Ramana Maharshi often told the allegory, The Tree of Awareness to illustrate this essential truth, which set the foundation for my shift into Being.

In this allegory, Bhagavan refers to a tree whose shade protects us from the intensity of the sun's heat, the heat of Ignorance. When our consciousness is at rest, we find ourselves under the shade of this tree. While we're protected from the sun's rays of Ignorance, however, we sometimes fall asleep into a dream of illusion. In this dream, we leave the shade of the tree. As real as the dream seems, it's not until we wake up from the dream that we realize we never left the shade at all.

But, if we're always figuratively under the shade of The Tree of Awareness, why don't we experience more equanimity and clarity in our daily lives? It seems it would be the most natural thing to rest as we Truly Are.

Then, when we fall asleep, the dream-illusion seems more real than Reality. How can that be? Our fears and desires are deeply imbedded in our psyche, and they are our primary motivators to action. Within the dream, our deepest fears and desires are played out, pulling us away from our True Nature.

For example, let's assume that in our dream, our peace under the shade of the tree is disturbed by a figure who is standing in the heat of the sun. It arouses our fear. It yells to us, "There's a fire to put out! You'd better get out from under that tree and handle this crisis!" All of a sudden, the heart beats faster, the mind races, and we run outside into the sun to put out the alleged fire. We handle the crisis and feel a tremendous sense of relief. But, that sense of relief is the hook that ensnares us to handle more crises.

Sometimes the dream has a different beginning. We start under the shade of the Tree of Awareness, but this time there is a figure of seduction, seducing us from under the tree. It says, "You think it is really a great experience under the tree, but here's one that is even better!" It does look better. And so, in this dream, we run out from the shade of the tree to experience this new, shiny bobble. But again, there's the ensnaring hook. Only this time, it is the wish to fulfill desire.

In both scenarios we stay in the sun, exposing ourselves to the heat of Ignorance. We forget we are in a dream; we continue to create more crises to feel the illusory relief and more desires to feel the illusory fulfillment. We stay in the sun. We get hot. We get dehydrated. And most of all, we forget that there is True Relief under the shade of the tree.

The end of Ramana's allegory is that we always awaken from the dream. A realization emerges: During the entirety of the dream, we never even left the shade of the tree. We were sheltered there the whole time. As real as the dream feels as we dream it, the moment we wake up, all is well.

We realize our error in perception. This realization is the *re-turning* to the Awakened state. The 'dream' in Maharishi's allegory is analogous to my 'foray into the mind.' The dream, like the foray, always comes to an end. As real as that foray seems at the time, the ending of the dream is guaranteed. The gift of being lost in the dream is that when we wake up, it reinforces *True Knowing* that we never left the shade of the tree. And that *re-turning* builds the foundation of the maturation into full self-realization.

CONCLUSION:
Beyond Awakening

"The heavy load you are carrying, isn't, and never was yours."
--Sri Ramana Maharshi

n Hinduism, Reality is called **"Para Brahmin."** Translated from the Sanskrit, these words mean, "beyond the spirit" or "universal self." Here, the separate sense of "I" is nothing more than a ripple in the stillness of Pure Love. It is considered to be That which exists before Consciousness, and out of which Consciousness arises.

Para Brahmin is the universe beyond the veils of this world, where Love impresses a divine design onto the fabric of the universe. Everything that has ever been, or ever will be, is created and moved by the divinity of this Grand Design. That means we can truly lay down our burdens.

Ramana Maharshi told a story about a man who, at his birth, is given a suitcase to deliver. He boards the train, and, as is the custom in India, he places it on his head. Once on the train, he believes that for him to deliver the suitcase he needs to carry it on his head. Throughout the journey, he dutifully carries the heavy suitcase on his head.

He carries it into the dining car, to his seat, and even sleeps with it on his head. His thoughts constantly return to the suitcase. He strategizes about different ways to relieve the weight. He takes workshops on how to cope with heavy weight on his head. He tries to ignore the luggage. He engages in spiritual practices to accept the heavy burden he constantly carries. Although it seems better at first, the new solutions never seem to work for very long.

Then, one day, an old friend boards the train with his own luggage and taps him on the shoulder. He says, "Why don't you just put that suitcase up in the luggage rack? The train will carry it nonetheless."

"Oh," the man reflects, "that never occurred to me."

He puts the suitcase up on the luggage rack and takes a seat, free from the burden of the suitcase and secure in the fact that the train will safely carry both him and his suitcase to his destination. His attention is now free from focusing on the needs of carrying the luggage. He finds the center, the calm in the eye of the storm.

As you mature into your Radical Awakening, the sense of the personal I, which is carrying the suitcase, begins to drop away. You find that the one who is doing the creating becomes less prominent. You begin to realize that the moment unfolds on its own, without your help. The train does not need you to reach its destination.

Within this realization lies the calm, the True Heart that is always there in the storm of life. You are always under the shade of the *Tree of Awareness*, even though you're dreaming that you remain in the hot sun. But, when you wake up, it is the shade to which you always return.

Papaji was frequently asked how best to approach life after an awakening, and how the awakened state could be maintained.

"I can answer that question using three words, two words, and one word:

Make no effort.
Do nothing.
Stop.

NOTES
How to Use the Audio Files Connected to this Book

*A*n exciting feature of this book is the audio files that correspond to each Step of the Radical Awakening. *Recording 1* is "The Warm-up" which you will be instructed to listen to in the text. Then all Seven Steps are included in the one audio file, *Recording 2, Your Radical Awakening,* and you are given instructions how to listen to this one audio file.

These audio files are accessed ONLY via a computer or mobile device (iphone, android or tablet) either by typing in the following URL or by using the Kindle App.

These recordings are stored in a folder in Dropbox, a webpage easily accessed through a few easy steps beginning with this link

http://tinyurl.com/jjwtqew

This link is the gateway to the area where these audio files are stored.

You will be directed to a webpage which will ask for your name and email address. Once that is entered, and you press "yes", a window will open with the link and password to the audio files folder. Please note down your password.

After selecting the "click here" button, you will be directed to the program, Dropbox, where you then enter the password and voila! you are in the **Kindle Audio Downloads** folder and the files are all there.

Now you have several options for listening

1. You can stream the files whether on a computer or mobile device. Simply select the file, double click or tap and play.

2. Download all the files for offline listening directly to your mobile device or computer

On a computer:

Download ALL CONTENTS IN THE FOLDER directly to your computer by selecting the Download button in the upper right corner of the site's page. A page will then load that will ask you to join Dropbox or sign in. Neither is necessary. At the very bottom of that screen you will see a message that states No thanks, continue to download →. ALL THE CONTENTS in the folder will then be downloaded to the downloads folder on your computer.

On a mobile device:

You MUST have the Dropbox App on your device. This requires you to sign up for a free account.

iphone/ipad users:

- Upon entering the Kindle Audio Downloads folder you select the ellipses (the dots) in the upper right corner and save to My Dropbox.

- the same window remains, select cancel and you are directed to the home page of Dropbox app.

- The folder is then accessed through the "files" button on the bottom toolbar.

- Tap to open the folder to make all files offline

- Tap the downward arrow next to a file to reveal a set of actions.

- Tap "Make Available Offline" and the file is automatically moved to the offline folder in the toolbar.

- Now you no longer need a wifi or data connection to listen to the audio

Android users:

- After selecting the "click here" button, a window open that will ask you what application you want to use.

- Choose Dropbox
- Kindle Audio Downloads folder will open with all the files.
- you select the down arrow next to an audio file and choose offline.
- The file is in the offline folder which is under the horizontal bars in the upper left corner of the window,
- Then tap the appropriate audio file and the player you want to use.

Should you need to use thehttp://tinyurl.com/jjwtqew link again do not worry. You will be directed to the first page, again, where you will need to reenter your email. HOWEVER you will then be directed to a page which states "You are already subscribed". There are two buttons one which is labeled "sign up again" and one says "Don't proceed". Select "sign up again" and you will be directed to the page to reenter the password that links to the audio files.

RESOURCES

Radical Awakening Website:

www.radicalawakening.org

Ramana's Facebook Profile:

https://www.facebook.com/RamanaNow

Ramana's Facebook Page:

https://www.facebook.com/RadicalAwakeningwithRamana/

Pilgrimage to Arunachala:

https://www.youtube.com/watch?v=7402hQKT364

http://radicalawakening.org/India/ArunachalaMenu.html

Buddha and the Gas Pump Interview:

https://www.youtube.com/watch?v=mMqHqpLSRgw&t=752s

Acknowledgments

When giving thanks to the people that helped this book come to fruition, it's hard to separate those particular individuals who supported the actual writing of the book from the people who generously supported the work of Radical Awakening with their love and energy. Since the Radical Awakening work continued to develop for twenty-one years, so too did the material in the book.

Although it is customary to cite your teachers and inspirations first in the acknowledgments page, I will acknowledge the people who supported and carried this work over the test of time, without whom my personal inspirations would not have gone beyond my tiny 350 square foot home in India.

My apologies in advance to those whose names I've neglected to include, and to those who have hosted me in their homes and worked behind the scenes since 1996. You allowed for Radical Awakening to be shared all around the world. Spanning the decades, the people who hosted me in their homes for weeks at a time worked behind the scenes so Radical Awakening could be offered in their town. Although too many to list, I want to thank every single one of you. You were the real torch bearers for Radical Awakening, whose flame is still be burning after all these years because of you.

But I would be remiss if I were not to mention Julie Marshon, who birthed and organized the first Radical Awakening Weekend Workshops in 1996 at my turn-of-the-century home in Boulder, Colorado. Julie believed in me and was the first to see the vision of this work.

And, it was the selfless love of Suzanne Taylor that took me out of my comfortable nest in Boulder to her beautiful Beverly Hills Mansion, bringing

Radical Awakening to Southern California. Suzanne had been hosting Marianne Williamson, Barbara Marx Hubburd and many other luminaries in her home, and I felt privileged to have been included.

The next category of people to whom I will be eternally grateful are the people who not only hosted me in their homes, as well as organized my two to three-week visits, but untiringly did so for many years, some almost a decade. These people became my family. That family includes Julia and Pierre Iachetti, HarinderDhillon, Bob Eagle in Victoria, British Columbia; Meg and Phil Watson, Jas Cheema and Kathy Pomeroy in Vancouver, British Columbia; Randall and Allana McFarlane in Encinitas, California; SudhaVanMunster, Sandy Plumb and Frank Dutko in Rochester, New York; Donna Gee in Hong Kong; Natec, Jenny White in Hawaii; and, Neil and Usha Hayward on Salt Spring Island, British Columbia. A special nod goes to Paulette and Chuck Elberti, whose invitation to me to hold a Radical Awakening Workshop in 2004, with their continued work and efforts, spawned a growing Rochester *sangha* (spiritual family).

I see as one of the great gifts in my life how all of you, both mentioned and not mentioned, supported me in your homes, so readily welcoming me into your family.

I cannot express enough thanks to the people who were instrumental in the actual writing of the book, whose contributions were immeasurably valuable. On the very top of the list are Beverly LaRock in San Diego and Kimberly Moekle from Los Altos, who spent hundreds of hours with me, shoulder to shoulder, working on one the most difficult tasks for an author: to speak what cannot be put into words, the direct experience of Consciousness. Beverly, a graduate of both Harvard and Stanford, and Kimberly, a lecturer in the Program in Writing and Rhetoric at Stanford, offered their professional skills as a love offering to further this work. My humblest gratitude goes to both of you. Most of the 'heavy lifting' was accomplished by these two editors.

As well, poet extraordinaire Lulu Love Rose welcomed me into her home for a month and worked shoulder-to-shoulder with me, and then continued work with me over Skype and Google Docs to give me her artistic flair to the book.

My thanks also extend to professional writing coach Ann McIndoo, who took my 1,100-page manuscript that was scattered everywhere, and stayed with me until it was paired down into concise chapters and topics. Another mention goes to Chris Boys in India, who joined me in 1997 to work on the first official draft of this book, and later in 2014, collaborated with me to polish the audio recordings accompanying with this book.

There were also the people who supported me by making the time and space available for me to sit and put words to paper. On the top of that list is my ex-wife, Antoinette Judelsohn, who lovingly did everything she could to give me the time to write throughout our twelve years of marriage; Rich and Leah Ashman, who paid for a rental in an ideal writing spot next to the ocean on the Big Island of Hawaii; Marushka, who funded my coaching program with Ann McIndoo; and last, but certainly not least, is Mardy Farrier, who has recently been my primary wingman. Mardy took on the seemingly impossible job of helping me organize my work and my life, and always picked up pieces that I just did not have time to get to-- who wouldn't want one someone like that in their life?

Just as it would be too numerous to list all of the people who have hosted me and selflessly worked behind the scenes supporting Radical Awakening, it would also be too long a list to cite all the teachers I have studied with over the past the forty-four years. But I do want to acknowledge the early influencers in my life, the people who 'showed me the path.' In 1968, it was Robert Frye who exposed me to Fritz Perls and invited me into a Gestalt Therapy group, which I attended five days a week from 1968 to 1969. Also in 1968, Stephan Gaskin, a hippie dropout professor at San Francisco State University, pointed me to Suzuki Roshi and the San Francisco Zen Center.

I feel that all of my ensuing teachers and life lessons finally brought me to Lucknow, India to study with my beloved Papaji. He was my last teacher and pointed me to his teacher, Ramana Maharshi (one of South

India's most loved modern saints), and then to my ultimate guru, a holy mountain in India called Arunachala. Ramana Maharshi stated that this sacred mountain contains within it a sacred flame that emits a powerful transmission, which silences the mind and opens the heart. I pray that this transmission saturates every page of this book and that you will find your way home to your true heart.

44903395R00099

Made in the USA
Middletown, DE
11 May 2019